THE LANGUAGE OF ETHNIC CONFLICT

THE LANGUAGE OF
ETHNIC CONFLICT

SOCIAL ORGANIZATION
AND LEXICAL CULTURE

IRVING LEWIS ALLEN

COLUMBIA UNIVERSITY PRESS
NEW YORK   1983

Library of Congress Cataloging in Publication Data

Allen, Irving Lewis
  The language of ethnic conflict.

  Bibliography: p.
  Includes index.
    1. Americanisms.   2. English language—
Etymology.   3. English language—United States—
Social aspects.   4. Nicknames—United States.
5. Epithets.   6. United States—Ethnic
relations.   7. Culture conflict—United States.
I. Title.
PE2831.A4   1982   306'.4   82-9610
ISBN 0-231-05556-0
ISBN 0-231-05557-9 (pbk.)

Columbia University Press
New York   Guildford, Surrey

Copyright © 1983 Columbia University Press
All rights reserved
Printed in the United States of America

Clothbound editions of Columbia University Press books are Smyth-
sewn and printed on permanent and durable acid-free paper.

CONTENTS

ACKNOWLEDGEMENTS

The makers of dictionaries, past and present, especially those who recorded the slang and disrespectable words of their day, are the providers for this study.

Several of my colleagues in sociology at the University of Connecticut read all or part of the manuscript in its various stages and gave me cheer. Among them, especially, I thank Mark Abrahamson, Michael Gordon, Josef Gugler, and Charles Logan for their advice. Harold Abramson encouraged me from the beginning and put many sources into my hands.

Friends of the project in other disciplines and other places helped as much. Especially, Polly Reynolds Allen gave much time to advise me well on every aspect of the project. Reinhold Aman generously corresponded with me about the study and led me to many sources.

The University of Connecticut Research Foundation awarded a small grant to launch the study and later supported typing and photocopying expenses.

THE LANGUAGE OF ETHNIC CONFLICT

INTRODUCTION

Let us hope that we will never grow so sanctimonious that we cannot listen to the mean things people say. They are our data.—Everett C. Hughes and Helen MacGill Hughes, from *Where Peoples Meet*, 1952, p. 132

Everyone knows that many terms of abuse for ethnic persons and groups have been used in the slang and other popular speech of American English. The existence and use of these words have been long and widely commented on, usually as evidence of prejudice and discrimination against minorities. Yet the substance of this vocabulary, as opposed to its spirit, has not been studied as a cultural response to an ethnically diverse society. Through the course of the nation's history, over a thousand names and hundreds of variants have been used for more than 50 different American groups. These words are abundantly recorded in scholarly records, particularly nineteenth- and twentieth-century dictionaries of Americanisms, but also in many other authoritative sources. The scholarly value of these terms is not self-evident. Their deservedly bad reputation has deflected attention from their usefulness as chronicles of social organization and change in American society.

In this study I use nounal epithets or generic nicknames for ethnic persons in American English as research data to address one of the oldest questions in sociology. How do objective demographic and ecological situations in communities generate culture and, in this case, a lexical culture? The vocabulary of ethnic abuse is a response to social diversity and it is elaborated by the effects of population size and density. While also a product of conflict in small towns and rural areas, as in the nineteenth-century South, name-making and name-calling proliferated in the close quarters and conflictful contacts of big-city life. The majority of the terms for European groups entered the language in response to the great immigrations and the churning effects of the industrial city, especially from about 1880 to 1930.

The language of ethnic conflict includes majority vocabularies of social control and minority vocabularies of resentment and protest. Nicknames for ethnic groups are clearly a vocabulary of instrument by which people and groups in communities express, reinforce, and redress rank orders along ethnic lines. The size, variety, and emotionality of this vocabulary is a "phenomenon," both in the sense of a universally observable event resulting from cultural contacts and in the other, popular sense of a spectacular and remarkable thing. Yet whole books are written on the stereotypes of national character, ethnic prejudice, and intergroup relations with little or no mention of the existence of the world of words spawned by those relations. Certainly, some think that ethnic slurs are too transparent in their meaning and not that important in and of themselves. But insofar as the grist for the sociological mill is the ordinary stuff of everyday life, then the vocabulary of ethnic conflict is singularly neglected.

Lexicographers, dialectologists, and, occasionally, folklorists have collected most of these American words and studied their uses and origins. I think first of H. L. Mencken and his early notes on terms of ethnic abuse in *The American Language,* beginning with the early editions. One of Mencken's great contributions was to emphasize the influence of immigrant groups on the words and ways of American English, by way of both the new words invented by them in response to their new settings and the new words coined by others to name the newcomers, always pejoratively. Mencken's arch attitudes toward ethnic minorities—and, for that matter, toward majorities—are well known; he could not resist using a few mild epithets even as he wrote with scholarship of others. His work on nicknames for ethnic groups has been carried forward to abundance by at least two generations of scholars, most of whom are cited in the chapters that follow. I would like to think that Mencken, wherever he is, would smile on further work on this sinful and homely vocabulary. My first task was merely to cull these many names from dictionaries and word lists of American slang and dialectal English and from many other scattered sources. Then there was the other matter of making sense of it all.

As a sociologist, I came to these lexical data by way of an interest in the cultures of urban communities or urbanism. These cultures include the whole range of behavioral adaptations and cultural responses, including language, to the objective situations of life in cities, suburbs, and towns. Louis Wirth, summarizing in the late 1930s the teachings of the Chicago School of urban sociology, wrote that urbanism resulted from the direct effects of population size, density, and variety. These early sociologists believed that the effects of city life on the traditional community were at once disintegrative and assimilative and, generally, represented a devolution of social organization. Sociology is still struggling with the ambiguities of this legacy in such value-laden questions as the best balance between ethnic pluralism and assimilation in community life. The Wirthian hypothesis is now much modified and qualified, but there is still value in finding new ways to verify the effects of social organization on culture. The names that ethnic peoples have called one another are, I believe, useful data to corroborate and even to clarify what we know about the social processes of structure and change.

This vocabulary, I shall argue, arises from cultural contact, especially in cities, and is aggravated by inequality, perceptions of competition, and the forces of market society. As I collected these words, I saw patterns that signified more than just so much interpersonal and intergroup prejudice and stereotyping. The history of how, when, and where the words were coined affirmed my decision to leapfrog the usual interpretation, which stresses the present subjective uses of name-calling, and to ask after the sources of this vocabulary in the past objective situations that seemed to generate it most profusely. I soon realized that the broad outlines of historical and present relations among and within ethnic groups are revealed by the referents of these terms, the dates of their entry into American English, and the numbers of terms aimed at different groups. Minimally, I think this study will show that this vocabulary is larger, more varied and involving of all groups, and more a product of objective situations, than is often supposed.

Ethnic slurs and epithets are, of course, the symbolism of stereotyping and prejudice, and they are used ideologically to justify discrimination against minorities. The uses of this vocabulary as weapons—the hurling of epithets—is rightly regarded as a social problem and one that has deleterious consequences for its victims. For at least a half century, a good part of American sociology has been devoted to studying and often condemning this behavior. Paradoxically, not too much, yet little more, can be said about the inaccuracies of ethnic stereotypes, their insidiousness, and the evils that hatred and racist theories have released and continue to release.

Many of the slurs are genuinely offensive and will strike some persons of ethnic sensibility as obscene—an outrage to human dignity. They may feel that it is fulsome to recount every known term of abuse in the language, that it is enough to know of their lamentable existence. As these words are aggregated and organized in this study, they certainly seem a squalid litany. Many among ethnic minorities are smarting from great and recent injustices and some among the majorities are deeply sympathetic. There is a lot to be said for not mentioning rope in the house of a hanged man. These Americanisms are sometimes ugly words, but they are our words.

The reluctance of social scientists to deal extensively with abusive words for ethnic groups may stem, in part, from an ambivalence about the ancient issue of the balance of conflict and consensus in society and from the new issue of the false alternatives of ethnic pluralism or assimilation. To dwell on the symbols of divisiveness may to some intimate an untoward acceptance of divisiveness, for the popular ideology of pluralism stresses the harmoniousness of intergroup relations over their conflictfulness. Yet, sociologists now understand that conflict and consensus are complementary and that both will remain central to the workings of American society as long as we remain diverse and find personal identity in the particulars of diversity.

As I collected these words and studied their origins, semantics, and uses, I wondered whether they are better thought of as the cultural residue of a national tragedy or just the seriocomedic side of American life. Whatever their high meaning, they do give a retrospective, yet immediate and pungent, sense of the bitterness, pathos, and desperation of ethnic conflict. I was struck first by their viciousness and triteness and sometimes, finally, by their low comedy. Genteel philologists have relegated this vocabulary to the order of profanity, and its meaning in American life has been ignored. This vocabulary is too often read only as malice and too seldom as folklore with all the inventiveness, ideological utility, and inadvertent confession of other folklores. I hear in these words more than the din of billingsgate. They are, above all that, the echoes and re-echoes of historical situations, of issues wrangled over, and of the very incidents of contention.

This is a study in sociology, not in lexicography. I have not recorded a previously unrecorded word, antedated a word, or resolved a difficult etymology. My work, rather, has been to gather in the terms and to juxtapose them in ways that illuminate their social origins. In this light, the etymologies and semantics of the words are sometimes clarified. I hope, as a sociologist, that I have correctly interpreted these rich lexical data.

Storrs, Connecticut
December, 1981

CHAPTER 1 **NICKNAMES FOR ETHNIC GROUPS**

If we had a complete history of all the words which America has preserved, invented, or modified, we should possess the most revealing history conceivable of the American people.—Robert L. Ramsay, 1880–1953

Ordinary ethnic slurs, especially nicknames, are extraordinary chronicles of historical situations that produced and reproduced prejudice against groups and increased social distance from them. Over a thousand usually derogatory terms for more than 50 American groups have been accumulated in scholarly records of slang and of dialectal English. The accumulation of nicknames for a group reflects the quantity and quality of that group's past relations with other groups.

This is only seemingly contrary to the common sense that verbal abuse reflects only prejudice. Actually, it shows that both prejudice and verbal abuse heap in reaction to the history of a group's conflictful contacts with other groups. The social antecedents of these often offensive words corroborate the social conflict perspective on intergroup relations. These words also show something of the dynamism of ethnic diversity and document the strains of assimilation. In what seems a paradox, the stereotypes generated by the plural society underscore its great diversity.

An elementary fact about the relation of language to society is the twofold proposition that language reflects social organization and that language constrains social cognition of society (e.g., Hertzler 1965:34-37, 100-16; Fishman 1972:155-72; and others). The vocabulary of nicknames for ethnic people in American English is an inventory of outgroup stereotypes and so constrains the perception of people who use them; this has been the main interpretation of ethnic epithets. The related proposition that language mirrors social organization is of greatest interest here. Fishman (1972:166) writes, "In a very real sense a language variety is an inventory of the concerns and interests of those who employ it at any given time." The array of nicknames for an ethnic group that have been used in a language indicates how much and in what ways that group historically has concerned other speakers of the language. The historical inventory of these words is a remarkable example of the reflection of society in language.

The normative conventions of social science have discouraged the study of ethnic epithets, except as devices for stereotyping and as indexes of prejudice. Little more can be said about the moral offensiveness of these labels, their stereotypical inaccuracies, and their sometimes deleterious consequences for victims. Theory and research in the area of intergroup relations and their cultural artifacts have reflected—and to an extent still reflect—preoccupation with the normative concerns about prejudice and discrimination and with minority groups as victims (Schermerhorn 1970:6-9). Also, a psychologized perspective has dominated studies of the aggressive and abusive language of intergroup conflict, which sometimes seem to assume that ethnic stereotypes and derogatory names spring almost spontaneously from the malice of prejudiced people. The venerable and somewhat tautological observation that ethnic stereotypes, such as abusive nicknames, express ethnocentrism has almost precluded alternative analyses. But sociology also has an interest in exploring the objective situations in society that produce ethnocentrism.

This study has two interrelated aims. The first is to use the accumulation of ethnic nicknames in American English as new, historical data to evaluate the proposition that ethnocentrism and the variety of names for outgroups that express prejudice and stereotypes are serial consequences of specific political, economic, and especially demographic situations. Attitudes of bigotry and racism (and the vocabulary that has expressed them) appear as intervening variables between structural situations and acts of overt discrimination against victims. The symbolism, the stereotypes, and often the etymology of the names display the substance and tenor of intergroup struggles over resources, cultural influence, and status. In short, the vocabulary produced by past social situations can tell us about those situations and also about the tendency for similar situations to produce similar results in any historical period and, by implication, in any society. The second and related objective is to explain with a social or structural theorem the cultural phenomenon of this huge class of words. This excursion into lexical analysis occupies much of the study. Both objectives are equally important, for the study explores society through language and language through society.

The pursuit of both goals requires a wrenching around of traditional thinking about the social meanings of abusive nicknames for ethnic groups. They are most fruitfully viewed as a kind of folklore of intergroup relations that rationalizes ideological beliefs about other groups and characterizes the relationships. The large size and the many targets of this vocabulary suggest an enormous and varied historical awareness of ethnic diversity in American life. Its size and variety also underscore the extent to which outgroup ethnicity and conflict have been nearly an obsessional undercurrent in American life and culture. Ethnicity, in fact, may be the largest single social theme in North American slang and popular speech. More than a thousand words and hundreds of variants denominate ethnic and quasi-ethnic entities and many others name the stations of ethnic change and emergence. Nicknames for American ethnic groups, cumulated historically, display not only the broad outline of our collective image of ethnic reality but also, remarkably, the detail and nuance of that image.

ETHNIC GROUPS

The names denominate members of more than 50 specific ethnic groups. Each group is an outgroup for name callers, who usually belong to some other ethnic group—their ingroup. An ethnic group can be succinctly defined as any racial, religious, language, national-origin, or regional category of subculturally distinct persons, regardless of the group's size (minority or majority), power (subordinate or dominant), or generational status (immigrant, native-born, or indigenous). Individuals may be members by birth, by personal identity, or by the ascription of society. Ethnically marginal persons may identify and be identified with two or more groups. By this definition, almost everyone is a member of some ethnic group. The only exceptions are ethnically nondescript persons, probably less than a tenth of the population, who have no ethnic identity, identities, or identifiableness, except as "American."

A popular but incomplete definition of a term of ethnic abuse is an appellation that members of the native-born white majority apply to members of a racial or immigrant minority. This stems in part from the euphemistic use of "ethnic group" as a low-income, oppressed, or recently arrived immigrant group. Hughes and Hughes (1952:137) pointed out this definitional error involving the semantic shift of the word *ethnic* to mean those groups who are not "charter members" of the community and who differ from the dominant majority and, lately, from whoever identifies with the majority. That is, this idea of ethnic group erroneously implies only minority status. This popular meaning has been rejuvenated and narrowed by the ideology and rhetoric of the recent white ethnic revival; only certain minorities are said to be "ethnics." (See Howard 1977:26-27, on the history of the word *ethnic*.)

Many people are not yet accustomed to thinking of ethnic majorities as just other ethnic groups. Actually, the white Protestant majority in the United States is not a single ethnic group but several quasi-ethnic entities. When individual white Protestants do not identify with a particular national origin, which surprisingly many do, they are often members of quasi-ethnic or subculturally distinct groups cut along regional, class, and denominational lines. White Southerners are the largest, most clearly defined of such groups, but there are others. For the same historical, situational reasons that other groups have been nicknamed, white Protestant groups have been nicknamed with a great variety of terms. Similarly, other large racial entities are not always of one ethnic group. Among blacks or Afro-Americans in the United States, there are many West Indians, Haitians, and other groups. Native American Indians and Eskimos are of many different ethnic groups. And the same is true of several national-origin groups.

NICKNAMES AND OTHER ETHNIC SLURS

The generic, common nouns of nicknames are but one form of interethnic verbal aggression, which is also expressed in language in a variety of other ways, such as in sayings, rhymes, songs, jokes, riddles, and other devices. There is no standard term that denotes all these expressions, except "ethnic slur." Some folklorists use the French *blason populaire*, which has no English equivalent. Roback (1944:251) coined the term *ethnophaulism*, from two Greek words meaning "a national group" and "to disparage," to refer to all types of ethnic slurs. All kinds of ethnic slurs in language originate in the same social processes and prejudices. Different kinds of slurs against particular groups are probably correlated in their incidence—a group that is frequently slurred in one way is frequently slurred in all ways. My impression is that blacks, Jews, Irish, Italians, Mexicans, and Chinese, who will be seen to have the greatest variety of nicknames, are most variously abused by other devices as well.

A brief review of ethnic slurs other than nicknames will serve to set them apart at the outset. First, the proper names of groups have been changed into scores of derisive adjectives (Cray 1962, 1965; MacMullen 1963; Tamony 1965; Porter 1966, 1967; and Monteiro 1968). Second, ethnic derogation appears in metaphors, such as *Irish spoon* for a shovel, *Italian perfume* for garlic, *Dutch steak* for cheap hamburger, *Jewish flag* for a dollar bill, *Chinese B* for an unearned grade in college, *Mexican carwash* for leaving a car in the rain, and many others. Third, names have been converted to derisive verb forms, such as *to dutch, to french, to nigger* (also *to nigger-out*), *to out-yankee, to welsh, to gyp, to jew* (also *to iky*), *to jap*, and *to scotch* (e.g., Eisiminger 1979). Fourth, ethnic slurs appear as "ethnicons" (Algeo 1977), another kind of metaphor, such as *swede* for a blunderer, *turk* for a cruel, aggressive person, or for a sodomite, *arab* for a footloose person, *scotchman* for a miserly person, *welsher* for a reneger, *pole* for a dumb person, *indian* for a reckless person, *tartar* for an intractable person, *hessian* for a mercenary, *yankee* for a swindler, and others. Fifth, slurs appear as proverbs (Roback 1944) and taunting exchanges in children's rhymes and sayings (Opie and Opie 1959:345; Porter 1965). Finally, ethnic slurs appear in narrative forms, principally the ethnic joke.

The joke is the most prevalent form of folklore in modern society, and the ethnic joke is one of the most common types, especially the popular "numbskull" jokes and riddles (e.g., Simmons 1966; Welsch 1967; Dundes 1971). Ethnic jokes are often blank checks in which the names of various groups are substituted according to the prejudices of the moment and of the company. Abrahams (1980) argues that the faddish ethnic jokes have undergone a changed social significance in recent years. They are no longer really directed at, or meant to be exclusionary of, their nominal targets. Ethnic jokes, he says, depict cultural differences as eccentric rather than deviant and "operate on the principle of the acceptability of cultural pluralism."

Of the various kinds of ethnic slurs, nicknames for ethnic persons and groups are the most numerous, varied, history-laden, and recorded. They are also eminently countable.

I have chosen to call these usually abusive and slurring nounal epithets simply nicknames, though to some it will seem too neutral a term for such censurable sentiments. *Epithet* is a good word meaning "to put a word upon" or "to call a name," especially a disparaging one. But in usage *epithet* includes a variety of devices other than names. *Nickname* denotes the particular device of nounal epithets, yet does not emphasize the linguistic process of pejoration, the social psychological process of stereotypy, or the social problems of prejudice and discrimination. The term *nickname* also distinguishes the illegitimate generic name for a group from the legitimate proper name.

The word *nickname* comes from Middle English *nekename* and means an appellative added to, or substitued for, the proper name for a person, often in ridicule, derogation, or just familiarity (Franklyn 1963:ix-xx). Before the thirteenth century, surnames were unknown, and nicknames were often added to help identify a person, like "Long" John, and this is still done in jest. Morris and Morris (1977:399) describe how the word *nickname* emerged. "These [tags] were first called *ekenames*—the *eke* meaning 'also or added.' Through a fairly routine linguistic change, 'an *ekename*' became 'a *nekename*' and eventually 'a *nickname*.'"

It is almost regrettable that Samuel Johnson was in error with his folk etymology that *nickname* is related to French *nom de nique*, roughly, "a name of contempt or derision," for it would agreeably suggest that nicknames of every kind are to some degree pejoratives. Francis Grose (1785:114) accepted Johnson's etymology and explained that "Nique is a movement of the head to mark contempt for any person or thing." Farmer (1889) said *nique* is an old cant word for "contemptuous indifference." Dr. Johnson's definition of *nickname* would be especially fitting for outgroup nicknames: "A name given in scoff or contempt; a term of derision; an opprobrious or contemptuous appellation."

Nicknames for ethnic persons and groups are a special case of nicknaming in general. A personal nickname, which is an informal proper name, denotes a category whose number is one, a personality. A different order of nickname is sometimes given to groups and aggregates whose number is greater than one, such as the many nicknames for residents of particular states. These are generic nicknames that are applied to any one or all persons of a group. An ethnic nickname, which is of this order, can be applied to any one person of a group, such as calling a particular Mexican person a *spick*, or it can be applied to the whole group, referring to Mexicans in general as *spicks*.

Ethnic nicknames, because of their origins in cultural contact and often conflict, are usually but not always derogatory.

While *nicknames* may be the best single term we have for nounal epithets for ethnic persons and groups, I will in the following chapters also use near synonyms such as *slurs*, *epithets*, and other terms as the context suggests.

THE SOCIAL PROCESS OF NICKNAMING

Franklyn (1963:xiii-xiv) observes that personal nicknames, as they occur traditionally, are often references to personal appearances, physical characteristics, occupations, season of nativity, or incidents with which a person or his ancestors were connected. Nicknames for persons are substituted by other people for the proper name in response to social images of the nicknamed person. Similarly, nicknames for ethnic groups are substituted by other groups for the proper name in response to stereotypes of appearance, national character, putative behavior, and so on. Nicknames for persons or for groups are added, not at the beginning of their life, but later in the course of life histories in response to experience and situations. The society of children, it is often noted, is in many ways a microcosm of adult social worlds and nicknaming among children is an instructive parallel.

Morgan, O'Neill, and Harré (1979) studied the social significance, formation, and uses of personal nicknames among school children. The process parallels the formation and uses of nicknames among ethnic groups, for both are cases of the phenomenon of nicknaming, which in turn is a case of naming in general. The authors show that children's nicknames derive etymologically from *internal* and *external* formations. Internal formations are rhymes, contractions, verbal analogues, and suffix additions. Many nicknames for ethnic groups also are word plays, alterations of the proper name, and shortenings, and use diminutive suffixes. External formations of children's nicknames are recognition of personal qualities (either physical, intellectual, or of character), of famous or striking incidents in school life associated with an individual, or of cultural stereotypes associated with a child's name; they may also be nicknames associated with certain proper names. Nicknames for ethnic groups similarly derive greatly from physical traits, putative national character, or great events, such as wars, and draw inspiration from the cultural stereotypes of folklore and mass media.

Morgan, O'Neill, and Harré go on to analyze children's nicknames as having social uses in the school society. These are remarkably close to the uses served by nicknames for ethnic groups in larger arenas, such as the community and the nation. First, children's nicknames serve to create and maintain social class. "People" are segregated from "nonpeople"; privileged groups are set off and their privilege is acknowledged and reinforced; and scapegoats are created. Second, children's nicknames promulgate and enforce social norms by highlighting deviations from the norms of physical appearance and behavior and, in doing so, indicate what those norms are. Nicknaming works by stigmatizing deviant individuals and the deviant trait and by creating pressures to bring behavior into line with the norms. It works by forcing the person to deal with the stigma, which is sometimes by self-loathing. Peter Opie (1970:355), the folklorist of children's lore, wrote that the well-known doggerel on name-calling should be rephrased: "Sticks and stones just break my bones/ It's words that really hurt me."

Similarly, anthropologists know that personal nicknames are used in other cultures for social control and to enforce conformity and that these nicknames reflect and dramatize central values in a culture (e.g., Antoun 1968; McDowell 1981). The nicknames for ethnic groups in the United States, and for that matter in any society, abundantly show that they are used to create and maintain social class and status and are an effort by majorities to exert social control.

THE SOCIAL AND IDEOLOGICAL USES OF NAME-CALLING

Every modern language has hundreds of disparaging nicknames for contacted ethnic outgroups. These terms reflect long histories of war, foreign occupations, and international trade (Roback 1944; Müller 1973). American English may have accumulated more nicknames than other modern languages because of the society's earlier and greater ethnic diversity, the historical prevalence of the competitive ethos, the comparatively high level of industrialization, greater social and geographic mobility, and the high utilization of technology—all of which have produced many points of contact and conflict among groups (e.g., Sagarin 1962:39). Moreover, the grammatical structure and semantics of the English language make it particularly conducive to vocabularies of prejudice (Ehrlich 1973:21-22). And slang is particularly serviceable as a vocabulary of aggression and prejudice.

Words are weapons; and "hurling" epithets is a universal feature of hostile intergroup relations. Outgroup nicknames are preeminently a political vocabulary. Name-calling is a technique by which outgroups are defined as legitimate targets of aggression and is an effort to control outgroups by neutralizing their efforts to gain resources and influence values. For majorities, name-calling justifies inequality and discrimination by sanctioning invidious cultural comparisons. That is, nicknames are a device that helps produce and maintain social class and privilege. For minorities, name-calling, in addition redresses social injustices and dignifies an imposed minority status and thus is sometimes a form of accommodation to conflict. It is an ideological process of naming devils to explain past and present injustices and to make sense of a complex and indifferent world.

Name-calling also serves to generate and maintain social cohesion and to demarcate boundaries between conflicting groups. The conflict implied by defining a hostile, monolithic outgroup helps to heighten ethnic identities and to strengthen traditionalism. Outgroup nicknames serve to define, to maintain, and to rationalize boundaries between groups and to stigmatize individuals who cross those boundaries by assimilation. In recent periods of rapid social change and in a climate of egalitarian ideology, much of the name-calling by minorities is to censure those groups who are thought to frustrate minority attainment and to scold individuals within their own group who seek social mobility independently of the group.

Ethnic identity in diverse urban society is maintained against pressures to assimilate, in part, by a negating process of pejorative and invidious distinction. Name-calling serves to make clear and to reiterate demarcations against which one favorably mirrors oneself and one's group. Nicknames then are labels for negative reference groups; they are a device by which people know who they are not and thereby who they are. They know that they are not like this or that group, often by the criterion implied in a nickname. On the other hand, Dundes (1971) suggests the possibility that ethnic groups may draw part of their identity from ethnic slurs directed at them, including nicknames. Slurs may reinforce certain group values, insofar as the stereotypes have some basis in ethnographic fact.

All these social uses of nicknames also mean that the words themselves are full of social history and can tell some of that history. Nonetheless, the social problem of name-calling warrants mention at this point. Stereotypes often have real negative consequences for the self-concepts and sometimes also for the behavior of victims who conform to stereotypical images.

The Consequences of Stereotyping. There is a vast and venerable literature on the effects of stereotyping, which is abstracted here without tracing the well-known intellectual history of these ideas. The overt purpose of an ethnic epithet is to insult and to injure. But calling names is also an effort, whether quite consciously realized or not, to control the behavior of the disparaged group. This effort at social control by derogatory labeling is an effort to manipulate reality by the mysterious identity of the verbal symbol with the nonverbal fact. The belief is that if one can name or attach a label to an object, in this case, an ethnic individual or group, then one can wield power over it by simply calling its name. If the name is abusive, denigrating, scolding, or ridiculing, it is expected that this definition will elicit an appropriate response, such as causing the victim to cower, to be denigrated, to be scolded and thus to feel guilty, or to act out the prophecy of ridiculousness. Usually this prophecy is fulfilled in the eye of the beholder by selectively perceiving or misperceiving the real behavior of the group over which he seeks control. Yet the ensuing social process of labeling and stereotyping sometimes also leads to redefinitions of the relations among groups and sometimes ultimately has the prophesied effect upon the behavior and self-concept of the victim, a result that has been called "inauthentication."

The social psychological process of being controlled involves losing one's authenticity by acquiring a false image of oneself. The stereotypes conveyed by nicknames are one device by which some minority group persons are deindividualized or depersonalized. Minority group members accept many of the values of the society in which they live, including sometimes the stereotypical images of themselves. Blacks, for example, in the past had many nicknames for other ethnic blacks that were a system of color-caste coding and signaled an acceptance of one criterion of white racism. This and other examples attest to one of the tragic implications of name-calling—eventual self-derogation of a group. Not only do groups sometimes accept the strereotyped image of themselves, but sometimes they reinforce it by conforming to its behavioral expectations. They have then affirmed the other's image and are thus controlled.

On the other hand, minorities, particularly blacks, have resisted stereotypes in creative ways. Derogatory labels, including names such as *nigger*, through inversion, have been given positive meanings within the group (Holt 1972; Brearley 1973, especially editor Dundes' notes). Broader stereotypes, such as thievery, sexual abandon, childishness, and laziness, through conversion, are acted out as techniques of aggression and ridicule against whites (Abrahams 1970:60-82).

For these and other reasons, the subject of ethnic slurs is usually regarded, analytically, as a problem in social psychology and, normatively, as a social problem.

NICKNAMES IN THE AMERICAN LANGUAGE TODAY

Francis Grose's (1785) A *Classical Dictionary of the Vulgar Tongue,* perhaps the first lexicon to include epithets for ethnic groups, listed terms then in British use for the Irish, Scots, Welsh, Jews, blacks, Gypsies, Dutch, English Catholics, and not surprisingly the colonial Americans. Some of the words were adopted by North American speakers of English, and a few listed by Grose are still heard today. A few Americanisms are traceable to the 1600s, such as *nigger*, and to the 1700s, such as *redman*. Many familiar terms, such as *wop, mick, kike, coon, greaser,* and *chinee,* have nineteenth-century origins, while others, such as *limey, wetback,* and *skibby,* appeared early in this century. Many others are of recent origin.

Most older nicknames have fallen into obsolescence, and many are archaic and wholly obsolete, though they remain a part of the history of culture and are pertinent to this study. Yet many terms, as an oral tradition, have a remarkable ability to be transmitted from generation to generation, if they remain useful. Many old terms for ethnic groups are still to be heard in street slang, in uneducated speech, and in regional dialects. New words are regularly invented that reflect contemporary social changes and register new outgroup awarenesses. Because outgroup nicknames are part of a vital language, they change over time in their connotations and the social contexts in which they are acceptably used. Ethnic nicknames also vary greatly in derogation, ranging from the overtly malicious and vicious to the puerile and jocular. All are offensive to some degree to some people, and this depends upon the speaker, the hearer, their relationship, and the social context in which they are used.

Many or perhaps most nicknames originated in various subcultures and seeped more widely into general usage when the subcultures came in contact with more general cultures, often through the mass media. Words that are most likely to seep into wider use are the slang of the underworld and prisons, drug users, the military, show business, teenagers, and college students. Importantly, many terms originated with minority groups, including loanwords from the languages and dialects they spoke.

The Role of Mass Media. As the country in the nineteenth century became more industrialized and the cities more diverse, the mass media, beginning with minstrelsy and vaudeville, reflected more and more the concerns, the interests, and the social worlds of their mainly urban audiences (e.g., Toll 1974:160-94). The mass media have had a special role in creating a vitality and popularity of nicknames, especially since the mid-nineteenth century. The modern media both reflect and create popular culture, using and in some cases inventing nicknames. The use of these words in everyday speech has been long reinforced by, and reflected in, the public media of print, popular songs, radio, movies, and, most recently, television.

The mass media actively influence language by popularizing slang and argots and introducing new words into wider usage, as well as rejuvenating old ones. Television and movies, responding to the new candor about ethnicity that began around 1970, are reintroducing some of the old ethnic epithets. Archie Bunker was probably responsible for taking *junglebunny* and other terms off city streets and into suburban living rooms. The tough big-city cops of the television crime dramas have rehabilitated the old slurs *wop, greaseball,* and others.

Through nicknames, the reflection of interethnic relations in the media has a long history. Some etymologists suspect, for example, that James Fenimore Cooper invented several nicknames for the mouths of his characters, such as the bogus Indian word *paleface* and the epithets *crow* and *wooly-head* for blacks. Mencken (1944) thought the term *octoroon*, modeled on *quadroon* (see chapter 5) may have derived from the title of a stage play in 1861 by Dion Boucicault.

The late nineteenth century and the rise of urban culture saw an enlarged role for the mass media in popularizing nicknames for ethnic groups. Popular songs virtually gave the language nicknames for blacks, such as *rastus, moke,* and *coon,* by giving the terms enormous popularity and perforce a certain legitimation. There was a popular song called "Rastus on Parade," published in 1896 by Kerry Mills. Mencken (1945:635) says that "*moke* was thrown into competition with *coon* in 1899 by the success of 'Smokey *Mokes,*' a popular song by Holsmann and Lind."

Coon, as a slur on blacks, became greatly popular by 1900. Originally a term for a white rustic, by the time of the Civil War *coon* was being applied to blacks (Flexner 1976:54). The raccoon has long been a symbol of cleverness, and some think that by the late nineteenth century the term may have had some positive use among urban blacks, perhaps under the influence of minstrelsy. Mencken (1945:632-33) tells the story of how *coon* was popularized as an ethnic slur. In 1896, Ernest Hogan, a black, wrote a song, "All *Coons* Look Alike to Me," though he did not intend it as a slur. Hogan was "crushed and amazed"at the resentment the song caused among blacks. As the song became popular, it was widely interpreted as a slur. Mencken quotes Edward B. Marks in *They All Sang* that the refrain became fighting words in New York and whites whistled it in the vicinity of blacks as a personal insult. In 1935, Marks wrote, "Hogan became an object of censure among all the Civil Service intelligentsia, and died haunted by the awful crime he had unwittingly committed against his race." Hogan's song was followed in 1899 by "Every Race Has a Flag But the Coon," written by two white men. In 1900, two other whites, Jefferson and Friedman, wrote "Coon, Coon, Coon," and, says Mencken, "from that time forward *coon* was firmly established in the American vocabulary."

The dialogs of movies in the 1930s and 1940s were sprinkled with mild epithets complementing the ethnic stereotypes scripted by writers and directors and played by actors of the period. Some of the ethnic nicknames heard in the dialogs were taken from actual slang but others were just made up. For example, Robert Taylor, playing an American in *A Yank at Oxford*

(1937), derisively referred to the English as *beefeaters*, which actually has been a nickname for the English. In Frank Capra's *It's a Wonderful Life* (1946), Lionel Barrymore called Italian workers "a lot of *garlicky-heads*," which is perhaps the first and only record of this term. Sometimes euphemisms were used for harsher words, as when a character speaks of "a colored gentleman in the wood pile" in Irving Rapper's 1942 movie, *The Gay Sisters*. At least one movie title, Elia Kazan's *Pinky* (1949), starring Jeanne Crain in the title role, used a familiar term for a racially mixed woman. In Howard Hawks's screwball comedy, *Twentieth Century* (1934), a black butler was named Uncle Remus.

During World War II, movies helped revive and popularize many terms for the Germans, Italians, and Japanese, some of which were quickly applied to those national groups resident in this country before the war. To take a few of many examples, in *Somewhere I'll Find you* (1942), Clark Gable, having set out to Indo-China to find Lana Turner, referred to Japanese soldiers occupying Saigon as *japanese beetles* and spoke of "vermin" and the need for "pest control." In *Hollywood Canteen* (1944), Jack Benny introduced a short, stout, mustachioed orchestra conductor as *Mister Spaghetti*.

In the 1960s and 1970s, the movies rejuvenated many ethnic nicknames, sometimes with informed scholarship, to enhance period flavor, to create realism in dialog, and most profusely to dramatize the bigotry of characters. In *The Sand Pebbles* (1966), a movie set in the 1920s, Steve McQueen repeatedly referred to the Chinese as *slope-heads*. John Wayne, in one of his westerns, knowledgeably referred to a white rustic as a *peckerwood*, just as it was used before it became a black term for whites.

In television, Archie Bunker was the archetype of a bigot, and Americans learned and relearned dozens of pungent epithets from Archie's bad mouth. As with portrayals of nudity and sex, the media allow the use of ethnic slurs when they have "redeeming social importance" or when they are "integral to the story line." But like some nudity and sex in movies and television, some nicknames seem mischievously gratuitous.

Today, the mass media, primarily television, is the principal agent for diffusing old and new folklore. In addition, the media have inadvertently inspired a few nicknames such as perhaps that of the animated cartoon cat character "Sylvester" (a black term for whites), the title of a television series

"Mod Squad" (a derisive term for a couple, one black, one white), and even the name of an actor, Stepin Fetchit (which became a term for a black flunky), whose old films were seen by a new generation on television.

The American novel is well understood as a chronicler of social organization and change. The genre of the urban or city novel (Gelfant 1970)—novels set in cities and in which the city is also an actor—sometimes portray the ethnic diversity of cities and responses of characters to that diversity. Among novelists of the city, I think in this connection of Theodore Dreiser, John Dos Passos, James T. Farrell, and Nelson Algren. The characters in Dos Passos' *Manhattan Transfer* (1925) use the nicknames of ethnic groups around them in the diverse city. Farrell, in *The Young Manhood of Studs Lonigan* (1934), used many ethnic nicknames, some of which were carried over into the recent television adaptation of the novel. Algren used ethnic epithets in *The Man With the Golden Arm* (1949). Ethnic nicknames are a staple in modern realistic novels of other sorts, such as the detective stories of Raymond Chandler. More recently, John Sayles in *Union Dues* (1977) sprinkled ethnic nicknames into the speech of his working-class Bostonians. John Gregory Dunne's *True Confessions* (1977) has a narrator and main character who uses period epithets.

The best-known nicknames for ethnic groups have become metaphors for prejudice. The terms are being used ironically in book titles—sometimes just the single word—to signal the theme of prejudice and discrimination. Dick Gregory's 1964 book, *Nigger: An Autobiography*, is one example. Gregory reportedly said, wryly, "Now any time a white man says *nigger*, he's advertising my book." John Keeble titled his 1980 novel *Yellowfish*, a nickname for Chinese illegal immigrants. And there is James Baldwin's 1964 *Blues for Mister Charlie*. In 1977, there was notice of a popular music group, "Kinky Friedman and His Texas Jewboys." Giddy trends sometimes touch academe. In 1972, a series of college textboooks used the titles *"Kike!"*, *"Chink!"*, *"Mick!"*, and *"Wop!"* to dramatize that the subject was prejudice against each book's namesake. A leading professional journal of sociology, in the table of contents of a 1981 issue, introduced four articles, one each on blacks, Chinese, whites, and Native American Indians, with the waggish caption "4 on Red Skins—and White and Black."

In the nineteenth and early twentieth centuries, ethnic nicknames and other epithets were seen regularly in news and editorial writing. The press, until the end of World War II, used several genteel epithets, which were then considered appropriate. As late as the 1950s, regional papers on occasion deliberately printed *negro* with a lowercase initial or made a pejorative by attaching the suffix *-ess* to the proper name of a group, as in *Jewess*. Except with literary, dramatic, and academic license, the press and broadcast media now for the most part carefully avoid locutions that smack of being ethnic epithets. In an atmosphere of heightened ethnic sensibilities, even the Oxford English dictionaries have come under criticism for recording certain ethnic slurs (Burchfield 1980).

Writers of the media and academicians are part of the social processes of naming new social realities and they occasionally slip into usages, including a few nicknames, that eventually will be understood as words that characterize, as well as indicate, their referents. Many fewer such terms are used today, the targets are different, and the allusions are more apt to be coded, but a few epithets are still in good repute. Lately, there is a penchant among journalists and academics to make nouns from adjectives and combining forms, such as *ethnic, Hispanic, Afro-, and Anglo-*, in the scramble to indicate and sometimes to characterize new ethnic realities. All these media influences have kept, and continue to keep, nicknames for ethnic groups alive in American English.

CHAPTER 2 TERMS OF ABUSE AS CHRONICLES OF INTERGROUP CONFLICT

Familiarity breeds contempt.—Aesop, c.620–c.560 B.C., from *The Fox and the Lion*

The social uses of nicknames discussed above set the background for viewing them next as reflections of social organization and change. This chapter considers what amounts to a slang vocabulary of anxiety and aggression arising from structural strains in society—a lexical culture that responds to population size, population density, and social variety. These considerations are built on the early work of others. Most scholarly research on this topic is highly ideographic, such as etymological and onomatological studies of particular nicknames. Lexicographers over the years have compiled most of these words in specialized dictionaries, and these will be discussed in the next chapter. H. L. Mencken (1936:294-300; 1945:595-639) made the first major etymological study of nicknames for ethnic groups in *The American Language*, beginning with the early editions around 1920. The British lexicographers, Ernest Weekley (1932:154-66) and Eric Partridge (1933:3-9) also wrote early on English terms of xenophobia.

EARLY STUDIES IN SOCIAL SCIENCE

Social analyses of this vocabulary are few and far between. William Graham Sumner (1906:27-30) briefly described the common ethnic epithet as the verbal expression of *ethnocentrism*. Wilmoth Carter (1944), a sociologist, listed and classified certain terms by group target and by themes of derogation. A. A. Roback (1944), a psychologist, made the first major study of ethnic slurs or "ethnophaulisms," as he called them generically. Erdman Palmore (1962), a sociologist, made, to the best of my knowledge, the first quantitative analysis of nicknames for ethnic groups in a society. Kantrowitz

(1969), in a parallel study, analyzed the vocabulary of race relations in the microcosm of Joliet Penitentiary. Kantrowitz, speaking from the premise "that language and vocabulary in particular reflect man's social life," saw the origin of abusive nicknames in interracial conflict, intensified by the close contacts of prison life.

Palmore's (1962) study of the national macrocosm is an exemplar of the psychologistic model that takes ethnocentrism and prejudice as independent and nicknames as an ahistorical consequence. Because this is the prevailing view, let us briefly examine the logic of Palmore's analysis.

Palmore analyzed the determinants of 125 nicknames, which he selected as those used by the white Protestant majoritry to derogate minorities. He set out five formal propositions, and the main one states: "There is a close association between the amount of prejudice against an outgroup and the number of ethnophaulisms for it" (p. 442). Majority group prejudice, which he indexed by Bogardus's Social Distance Scale, correlated highly (Kendall's tau = .95) with the number of nicknames for each of nine outgroups.* Palmore wondered in print why there should be any statistical correlation between prejudice and ethnophaulisms since "greater hostility could be expressed and reinforced simply by repetitions of a small number of ethno-phaulisms or by using stronger ones" (p. 443). The two variables are not only interdependent, as he notes, but I will add that they are also two ways of saying the same thing. Palmore's correlation between social distance (or ethnocentrism) and the number of nicknames for groups masks the fact that objective historical situations are antecedent to both. Palmore, in effect, was measuring past *social conflict* with the Bogardus Scale (see Newman 1973:222-23). The variety of nicknames tells us more about the sociology

---

*Palmore's "almost perfect" rank order correlations between Social Distance and the number of ethnophaulisms may be inadvertently exaggerated by the nicknames of, and the similarity between, certain categories used for the calculation. First, most of the nine "groups" are not single ethnic groups but are broad aggregates, such as "South and East Europeans." Second, the correlation is increased further by the fact that the four categories that occupy the first four ranks of *least* Social Distance and that have the *fewest* ethnophaulisms are, for the most part, white Protestants. Palmore called these "Canadians," "British (English, Scots, and Irish [sic])," and "North Europeans (non-Germans)," and "Germans." The correlation, I am suggesting, may be among six effective categories rather than nine, and the correlation would be substantially weaker. Nonetheless, a correlation between a ranking by white Protestants of Social Distance felt from many *specific* outgroups and the number of ethnophaulisms used against those groups would produce a positive but substantially lower coefficient.

and history of intergroup relations than about prejudice against particular groups today.

CULTURAL ANXIETY, MALE SOCIAL WORLDS, AND SLANG

Many terms for ethnic groups have those ephemeral, flippant, and outlaw qualities that make them slang. The vocabulary of slang is fraught with words that reach for meanings beyond the locutions of standard language, which often fails emotional needs concerning some subjects. Standard English nouns denote a referent, whereas words of slang characterize the referent and, moreover, produce a rhetorical effect (Dumas and Lighter 1978). The number of slang words for various social objects indicates levels of cultural anxiety about taboo, embarrassing, and stressful subjects. Emotion-laden subjects appear in slang with great frequency and expressiveness. American slang is permeated with words for sexuality, drunkenness, food, excretion, violence, failure, and cheating (Flexner 1960; Maurer 1978). It is sometimes said (e.g., Legman 1966) that the social releases of sex, drunkenness, and crime are the most frequent themes in the slang of the English language generally. Flexner (1960:xi) notes the many counterwords in American slang, including ethnic slurs, that express dislike for the unlike and that serve to bond the users.

Outgroup ethnicity is a highly frequent object of American slang, reflecting the special strains of the greater diversity of American society. In informal American English, the historical inventory of names directed at all ethnic and quasi-ethnic aggregates approaches two thousand terms.

Nicknames for ethnic groups may be regarded as indexes of the cultural anxieties of interethnic contact and conflict. Labeling is a process of codifying elements of a socially constructed reality; this is a fundamental principle of naming and of lexical formation. New words are coined to denote newly emerging social objects and, in slang, to take account of their emotional meaning, such as that of anxiety arising from conflict and competition.

The maleness of recorded slang is notable (Flexner 1960). Carl Sandburg said that "slang is a language that rolls up its sleeves, spits on its hands and goes to work." Less metaphorically, slang is an effort to deal with and to control a male social reality. Historically, the use of all kinds of nicknames may have been more prevalent in male than in female culture (Franklyn 1963:xvii). But an historical study of women's talk about women's worlds may show this to be but another male bias of selective perception, attention, and recording. Men's speech certainly has been more studied than women's speech and, moreover, has been reported as though it were the speech of both men and women (Thorne and Henley 1975). Women have always had jargons and secret languages about their worlds and concerns. These vocabularies are usually distinguished from slang, but perhaps artificially. Yet Revens (1966:xxiv) asserts that the "evidence is that, generally, and always excepting secret languages, women use men's slang, or none." Ethnic epithets in particular are a slang of the marketplaces of field and factory. While women have always participated in these arenas, fewer women have been involved and many of those less actively involved.

There are other reasons why women, in their traditional roles, are less likely to use slang (Jespersen 1922:245-48; Flexner 1960; Thorne and Henley 1975). Trudgill (1972) speculates that women compensate for subordination by signaling their status with "proper" speech, which he says, is "particularly true of women who are not working." In addition, the use of rough, tough, violent language and swearing, including the use of ethnic epithets, symbolizes masculinity, or at least its blue-color stereotype. The use of slang to signal masculinity, and its avoidance to signal femininity, may be enhanced among lower status people where gender roles and the sexes are particularly segregated and where symbols of masculinity and femininity are particularly important (Thorne and Henley 1975).

Many terms for outgroups originated in the traditional world of work and as a result of men's greater and more direct exposure to the public, competitive, and ethnically diverse marketplace in pursuit of income, jobs, advancement, and status. The marketplaces, often those of the dense, ethnically diverse, industrial cities, spawned the intergroup encounters and anxieties expressed in words of abuse for ethnic groups. I venture that female use of ethnic epithets has been increased and prompted by commiseration and identification with male anxieties in the marketplace and that the use of ethnic epithets by women in this century has increased with the involvement of women in the labor force outside the home.

The maleness of the vocabulary of slang prompts another elucidating analogy to name-calling among ethnic groups. Nicknames for outgroups bear a relationship to ethnic group rivalries, resentments, and anxieties similar to that which words of sexual insult and sexually "dirty"words bear to relations between men and women in society. Traditional male roles create expectations that men will be successful competitors, aggressors, conquerors, and possessors, and indefatigable ones at that. The anxieties resulting from acting out these roles are expressed in hundreds of words for women, for sexual anatomy, and for sexual acts of all kinds.

Since they make up a vocabulary of anxiety and aggression, outgroup nicknames constitute a social and semantic parallel to the abusive language that men have used against women. Both are chiefly male vocabularies that display the strains of traditional roles. Epithets for ethnic groups, as a vocabulary of psychological aggression, share with gender epithets clusters of phonetic elements, such as the popping and guttural sounds of labial and velar occlusion, whose sound semantics perhaps universally or at least widely connote pejoration (cf. Wescott 1971; Miller and Swift 1977:109). Gender and ethnic insults are sometimes linked. When nicknames for ethnic persons have gender, it is often as not feminine and sometimes derogates specifically female roles in conjunction with the ethnic slur. Much sexual slang is also political, representing efforts to wield power over women. In this sense, abusive nicknames for ethnic groups share a kinship to the many pejorative and derisive words for women.

For both vocabularies, it is more analytic to consider the structural strains in society that produce these words than to see such words as merely displaying the chauvinism of the name-callers. The women's movement is an effort to reform or revolutionize traditional gender roles toward a pluralism of equality. In this spirit, there has been scholarly interest in analyzing the male vocabulary of abusing and trying to control women (e.g., Schulz 1975). A study of the terms of ethnic abuse, I am suggesting, will also throw cold water on the horrific power of ethnic name-calling.

The other pariahs of the American language are the taboo vocabularies of sex, excretion, and blasphemy. On the whole, these words have fared better than ethnic epithets as raw materials for social research. Scholarly interest in formerly taboo vocabularies increases with public enlightenment about sex and body functions and with secularization. Most would agree that demystifying and demythologizing the taboo words of sex, excretion, and blasphemy signify healthier attitudes toward our bodies and a simpler humanism. It is not as clear that the processes of social conflict are "natural" or that its bitter signs can be in the least bit enlightening.

NICKNAMES AS ETHNIC AND URBAN FOLKLORE

While the stereotypes of certain ethnic slurs have been analyzed as folklore (e.g., Dundes 1971), the mass of outgroup nicknames themselves and the social meanings that surround them are not usually thought of as folklore and, as far as I know, have never been so analyzed. Abrahams and Kalčik (1978) suggest finding folklore in the troubled relations of cultural pluralism, including the expressive forms of ethnic slurs. Nicknames for ethnic outgroups can be usefully viewed as nonnarrative elements of a folklore of ethnic groups in conflict.

This vocabulary shares certain traits and social uses of folklore. These words are still orally transmitted for the most part and are part of an ingroup oral tradition of stereotypes and other lore about contact and conflict with other groups. They are sometimes embellished with folk etymologies, which are best understood as parables or allegories. These specious etymologies are symbolic narratives with ritual situations of conflict, heroes, villains, and a moral point concerning ethnic relations. For a particular group, these stories may justify the use of the term or, for the victims, they may dignify the derogation of the nickname. Folkloristic etymologies are reviewed in chapter 6.

When the country was mainly rural in the nineteenth century and earlier, the nicknames and their semantics were mostly of rural culture and were elements of a rural lore. With the rise of the industrial city and, shortly, its burgeoning with the new immigrations after about 1880, the nicknames for ethnic groups became, in addition, part of urban folklore, and increasingly so in this century. Urban folklore is a cultural response to modern, urbanized, industrial, bureaucratic society. In the preceding chapter, I discussed the role of the mass media in the preservation and transmission of words for ethnic groups. The rise of the mass media is integral to the development of urban society. The mass media also extend and complement face-to-face and other primary relations of society. In this way, the media serve as a social integrative mechanism, as well as generating and maintaining conflict between groups. Nicknames for ethnic groups are among the many aspects of mass communication and, as such, can be considered particles of an urban folklore.

In the academic field of folklore, there is a growing acceptance of the subcategory of urban folklore (e.g., Parades and Stekert 1971) and even of the idea that it need not be orally transmitted (Dundes and Pagter 1975:xiii-xxii). The cultures that emerge from the close quarters and intergroup contacts of dense, big-city life are increasingly viewed as extensions of and complements to the culture of traditional, rural, or folk societies. Stern (1977) also argues for an acceptance of the idea of urban folklore and, generally, the view of folklore as "unofficial culture" rather than as remnants of peasant cultures. The historical inventory of nicknames for ethnic groups in American English is a measureable product of both the rural and urban phases of national development. To be sure, the appearances of these words are even cultural indicators of the rural-to-urban transition.

Several theoretical statements would seem to accommodate a view of outgroup nicknames as part of foklore. Abrahams (1980:390) summarizes the uses of folklore performances in ethnic boundary-making. In his words, "The lore of self-typing and stereotyping projects and reinforces intragroup and intergroup conflicts." And, "This complex of ways in which ethnic lore explores the subject of social and cultural differences has been an especially productive way of drawing on folklore as an index to the intensity of social stratification and the dynamic of intergroup relations." Other, more specific interpretations also seem to speak implicitly of the folkloric character of name-making and name-calling.

Jansen (1959) wrote that folklore is variously esoteric and exoteric. Alan Dundes, in a prefatory note to reprinting Jansen's article, said that ethnic slurs lend themselves well to this line of analysis. In Jansen's words (p. 46), "The esoteric applies to what one group thinks of itself and and what it supposes others think of it. The exoteric is what one group thinks of another and what it thinks that other group thinks it thinks." Nicknames for out-groups, it would seem, are elements or an exoteric folklore of a group or its taxonomy of the ethnic diversity around it. Jansen goes on to posit, and I paraphrase, that large size and salience of outgroups tend to generate exoteric folklore about them, and that their culturally dominant status is no bar to this. Others have developed the idea that folklore is a way that unlike groups communicate with one another, sometimes hostilely.

Folklore performances not only are communications within groups that serve to integrate, but also may be communications to other groups, expressing conflict and aggression, or communications within a group between persons of different identity, expressing efforts to stratify the group (Bauman 1972). The ritual of outgroup name-calling and the lore of stereotypes and ethnocentrism that accompany it, I am led to say, are something like a folklore performance between unlike groups of different identities. Ingroup name-calling, which is treated separately in chapter 5, expresses conflict between persons of different identities, specifically as hostility toward persons marginal to the group; it is clearly an effort to stratify the group. The dominant esoteric perspective among folklorists may have averted attention from exoteric lore of intergroup conflict, perhaps also from the vocabulary of conflict. Bauman argues that differences of identity, not only shared identity, can be the basis of folklore performance. He urges a reorientation in folklore studies so as to understand the exoteric as well as the esoteric social base of folklore.

Stern (1977) discusses the "functions of ethnic folklore," which strikingly resemble the social uses of nicknaming among children (Morgan, O'Neill, and Harré 1979) and among ethnic groups. He describes ethnic folklore "as a vehicle for the maintenance of social cohesion, as a manipulatory device for aligning oneself with certain ethnic networks while separating oneself from other such networks, and as a means of psychological adjustment to problems of ethnic dislocation" (p. 22). Stern argues that ethnic folklore is a technique of social control of deviant behavior and is an instrument both of social solidarity and of conflict and aggression. He concludes that "Ethnic folklore is thus a defense mechanism whereby individuals protect themselves against the painful effects of ethnic conflict" (p. 25). Name-calling in protest and, especially, the spinning of defensive folkloric etymologies are clearly efforts to ameliorate the anxiety of ethnic conflict.

The new ethnic folklore of the cities is in great part a response to new social experience, contact with multiple ethnic groups, and the personal experiences of resettlement (e.g., Stern 1977; Kirshenblatt-Gimblett 1978). Stern, in particular, urges the extension of folklore to comprise the personal experiences of resettlement and the use of folklore as a material to analyze "the dyanmics of ethnicity in urban settings" and as a consequence of human interaction. Many nicknames for ethnic groups and some of the folkloric etymologies, considered as elements of urban and ethnic folklore, chronicle troubled relations with multiple ethnic groups and the immigration experience.

CONTACT, COMPETITION, CONFLICT, AND CITIES

In this final section, building on the ideas of the social uses of slang and of ethnic and urban folklore, I will find the social source of nicknames, individually and aggregately, in intergroup contact and conflict. A direct application of the social conflict perspective (e.g., Coser 1956) explains variations in the numbers and themes of nicknames that have accumulated for various groups over the course of their struggle with all other groups to control the reward and value systems of society. The number of nicknames for each group indexes the relative variegation of awarenesses of a group in society. The general empirical hypothesis of this study is that the more prominent, various, multifaceted, sustained, and troubled the contacts among groups, the more different nicknames will be coined and used.

It is a theoretical principle that intergroup contact, competition, and conflict are the structural sources of ethnocentrism and prejudice (Cox 1949; Bernard 1951; Simpson and Yinger 1953; Hamblin 1962; LeVine and Campbell 1972; and others). That is, prejudice grows out of historical situations, particularly economic and ecological situations, which become political situations.

Hughes and Hughes (1952:130-44) understood that the tenor of intergroup contact is expressed in outgroup naming. The immediate goal of conflict between groups is to neutralize and injure one another, which is the intent of name-calling. Ideographically, many particular nicknames clearly derive from specific situations (see, e.g., Flexner 1976). The aggregate of this vocabulary more broadly displays the general structure and substance of past intergroup conflict.

The origin of most nicknames can be tied to great social changes in a society. Industrialization, urbanization, and even bureaucratization have created myriad situations and conflicts expressed in these words. Every American war, from the Revolutionary War to Vietnam, has generated nicknames for the enemy outgroup. In foreign wars, the enemy was also ethnically different, which probably itself elaborated the number of names.

(The Civil War may have generated fewer nicknames than the Mexican War.) Encounters with our indigenous peoples, colonialism, waves of immigration, the Reconstruction of the South and its economic aftermath, economic expansion and upward social mobility, the Great Depression, the farm-to-city migration, slowed social mobility, and other structural changes are the ultimate independent variables that account for this large vocabulary in American English.

Intergroup conflict is most likely to occur under specific social conditions (Newman 1973:112-17). In an objective situation of competition, intergroup conflict is directly proportional to the degree to which groups perceive each other as competitive threats to maintaining or altering the distribution of social resources and cultural influence. From the view that distributional inequities are produced, maintained, and reproduced by the stratification system of class and status, much intergroup conflict emerges as a struggle to maintain or to alter the stratification system and hence the distribution of income and the other systems of social reward. A prevailing ethos of competition and achievement in a plural society stimulates the emergence of conflict. A milieu of normative competition is intensified when it is of the zero-sum game mentality and is in a market situation where resources are limited or believed limited. The historically prevailing ethos of competition and achievement in American industrial development heightened intergroup conflict and as a result increased nicknaming.

The cities, often as not, have been the arenas for this conflict. Historians of urban America, particularly Kessner (1977), Bayor (1978), and Stack (1979), have described the situations and issues of conflict among European groups in Boston and New York.

Competition in American Economic History. The competitive ethos was especially strong and accommodated the needs of industrial capitalism during the period of great economic growth and industrial expansion from the Civil War to the Great Depression. Many terms for ethnic groups mirror the conflictful intergroup relations during this maturing phase of industrial capitalism and the social and spatial arrangements this system produced and reproduced. Mass immigration was related to the need for industrial labor. The most proliferous period of nicknaming white European groups, for example, was between 1880 and 1930, during the great immigrations from eastern and southern Europe, when these groups came into contact with settled groups, especially the Nativists, who perceived keen economic competition (Higham 1963). Equally important is the fact that minority groups were pitted against one another, especially in the dense urban arenas, where all groups called each other names.

Other nicknames reflect conflict both before and after the 1865-1930 period of great economic growth and immigration. Many terms are of more recent origin and reflect demographic shifts and economic and political realignments since World War II, such as internal migrations from farms and mines to the city. The social changes and discontents of the 1960s and 1970s similarly are expressed in new terms. And new immigrations from Latin America, Asia, and Europe prompt new nicknames and revive and sustain the use of old ones.

Urbanism. Ethnocentrism and its cultural particulars appear wherever groups meet, but in urban communities intergroup tensions multiply and intensify. Urbanism, as sociologists use the term, is the behavioral, organizational, and cultural consequence of population size, density, and social variety in cities. Population size is usually a necessary condition for high density and great social variety in urban communities. In ethnically diverse cities, density, which necessitates the proximity of groups, intensifies ethnocentrism, including its lexical culture. Also, the social fact of ethnic variety in a community, in conjunction with proximity, itself stimulates ethnocentrism.

Dense settlement patterns, particularly cities, create multiple points of contact, stimulate intergroup awareness, and heighten perceptions of competition. These sometimes lead to intergroup conflict. LeVine and Campbell (1972:68-71, 160-62), from a cross-cultural perspective, summarized the influences of proximity and visibility on ethnocentrism and intergroup conflict.

The most disliked strangers are those closest, particularly if they appear to be burgeoning in number and are, or appear to be, in competition. Social distance, in some part, is a consequence of spatial nearness. Proximity and visibility, as much as anything, stimulate prejudice against particular groups. Ethnic cultures respond in part to conflict by making folklore, including lexical culture. Pederson (1964) collected a profusion of nicknames used among the ethnic groups of Chicago, who, I note, lived in such proximity and high visibility.

At the same time, ethnic variety in cities stimulates ethnocentrism and its supporting cultures and, in doing so, creates the social distances that maintain and intensify the variety. Georg Simmel (1904), the early German sociologist of urbanism, believed that the antipathies among diverse social types in the close quarters and daily contacts of big city life served to maintain the distances and buffers that made coexistence or social pluralism possible. The sum of this conflict, Simmel seemed to suggest, is a form of urban sociocultural integration.

Fischer (1975), revising Louis Wirth's (1938) famous hypothesis of urbanism as a way of life, which was greatly influenced by Simmel, theorizes that the city, due to its size and concentration, "produces a diversity of subcultures, strengthens them, and fosters diffusion among them." Taking the special case of ethnic subculture, Fischer argues that the size and ethnic diversity of cities create pressures on ethnic groups, on the one hand to assimilate, but on the other, to intensify or at least to maintain cohesion and ethnic identity. New cultural contacts and the often resulting clash or opposition, for a time at least, reinforce traditional ethnic cultures. Fischer (1976:132) says that ethnic contact in cities produces "mutual revulsion" and increases ethnocentrism and so strengthens ethnic cultures. I will add that this seems to allow ethnic groups to bear diversity or pluralism.

Urban culture is emergent. Yancey, Ericksen, and Juliani (1976) and Taylor (1979) reorganized theory to argue that situations, often demographic and economic ones, such as structural isolation and competition, produce and reproduce ethnic culture. These situations almost always entail encounters with other groups, whether face-to-face or through indirect economic and social forces. Names for outgroups are chronicles of these encounters. And insofar as these encounters resulted in assimilation, another large vocabulary sets apart marginal persons and assimilators.

There is no doubt that urbanization and, then, urbanism universally result in semantic innovation. Epstein (1959) gives us a superb description of how the new experiences and new concerns of highly diverse ethnic immigrants to the emerging urban communities of the copperbelt in Northern Rhodesia, now Zambia, resulted in new words for new social objects. After noting the influence of the mass media—newspapers and magazines—

on linguistic innovation, Epstein writes that "One development of particular interest is the growth of a new vocabulary of personal abuse, much of which originated in a purely political context" (p. 334). These terms tend to be generalized, and "In times of social tension the use of such terms can be a powerful sanction in promoting social and ideological conformity" (p. 335). Epstein argues that prestige is the single common thread that runs through the new vocabulary of urbanism, including words for the town itself, beer drinking, occupations, country bumpkins, physical appearances (especially light color), and a few ethnic epithets. Epstein sees the effort to ascribe status through semantic innovation as a key to understanding the social organization of African towns. I will show in the chapters that follow that ethnic name-calling in American history is a similar effort to stratify groups in the local community and in the society by ascribing lower ethnic status and by using similar symbols of prestige, such as color, occupation, place of residence, and many other allusions.

Group Size. The absolute and relative size of ethnic groups is both a direct cause of and a proxy for the several other ecological causal factors that prompt contact and aggravate conflict, such as density of settlement, awareness of competition, and social and cultural prominence by force of numbers. Many studies have shown that group size is directly related to opportunities for intergroup contact. These contacts may be conflictful (Blalock 1967:143-89; Blau 1977:19-44) or they may engender intergroup liking (Laumann 1973:43, 45, 238-40), depending upon the context of the contact. Group size, then, should predict the number or variety of accumulated nicknames for ethnic groups, because, first, size has an independent effect on intergroup contacts and, second, size precipitates and proxies other ecological situations. Insofar as these contacts result in conflict, they also result in social distance, ethnocentrism, and prejudice, as well as their display in nicknaming.

AN OVERVIEW

Six propositions summarize at the outset the major findings and conclusions of the study:

(1) *The population size of ethnic groups (a proxy for the number of contact points and the amount of conflictful interaction among groups) predicts the*

number of nicknames that have accumulated for particular groups. The largest ethnic groups, including those who make up the white Protestant majority, have been called the greatest number of nicknames. And most groups have been nicknamed with a variety of terms in direct proportion to their relative size in the plural society. Not only does the number of different nicknames increase with population size, but the number of variants of many prototypical forms also increases.

(2) *Variation unexplained by size is accounted for by other demographic and ecological variables.* Historical outbursts of name-calling are associated with waves of immigration, settlement patterns, concentration in cities, group occupational specialization, and internal migrations.

(3) *The nicknames document an awareness of the subcultural distinctiveness of quasi-ethnic groups, especially those cut along regional, class, and denominational lines.* Quasi-ethnic groups, which are products of long, postimmigration experiences, are as likely to be involved in intergroup conflict as the more recent immigrant groups. Regional groups (Southerners and Yankees) and, to use Gordon's (1963:51-54) neologism, "ethclasses" are profusely nicknamed, commensurate with their relative size. The awareness of these quasi-ethnicities as outgroups underscores their structural isolation and suggests the competitive process by which their ethnic character emerged. A general awareness of an ethnic culture in society and the existence of names for it also signals that it exists as an ethnic culture.

(4) *Almost all outgroup nicknames are highly specific of their targets, referring to over 50 specific ethnic entities.* Relatively few intraracial nicknames refer to broad categories of religion or regional origin. The high degree of subcultural specificity in the historical accumulations suggests that ethnocentrism and prejudice do not stem from a categorical rejection of the culturally unlike, but are the result of specific conflicts between specific groups, often over specific issues.

(5) *The symbols of outgroups reflected in the stereotypes of nicknames make clear that intergroup conflict has to do with struggles for cultural influence, distribution of resources through class and status, and redressing resentments of an imposed hierarchy among ethnic groups.* Depreciation of outgroups by nicknames is mainly in terms of nonphysical or cultural differences, even between racially unlike groups. All nicknaming is basically an effort to assign lower status to outgroups, sometimes by simple force of nominal

derision. Conflict in the plural local community is reflected in nicknames that assign low status by reference, for example, to stigmatized occupational roles and ecological niches. Psychological explanations of racism emphasize notions about differences in intelligence, but this is the allusion of only a few nicknames for racial minorities; allusions to low intelligence are as frequent among names for white groups.

(6) *Other nicknames denominate marginal and assimilating persons and document the process of ethnic variegation.* There are many words for descendants of racially unlike groups and for persons who are assimilating within their own lifetime or between generations. These deviations and departures from ingroup norms are scolded through use of reproving and derisive nicknames that stigmatize personal appearances and behaviors. The words document the strains of ethnic change and emergence.

CHAPTER 3 **THE HISTORICAL LEXICON OF ETHNIC EPITHETS**

Much of the slang-maker's skill is spent on foul ideas, which make the Slang Dictionary, at its best, an unpresentable book; while short of this limit, there is an ugly air about lists of words so largely coined by vagabonds and criminals, whose grotesque fancy plays fitfully round the real wretchedness of their lives....—E.B. Tylor, "The Philology of Slang," in *Macmillan's Magazine,* April 1874

This chapter has the straightforward but considerable task of classifying, listing, and annotating more than one thousand nicknames used for 57 ethnic categories, including about 50 specific ethnic groups. As defined earlier, an ethnic group is any racial, religious, national-origin, language, or regional category of subculturally distinct persons, regardless of size, power, or generational status. This word list is more than twice as long as any previous compilation of these terms. The list aims to exhaust the terms that, over the past two centuries, have gained enough use to be noticed and published in scholarly records of American English.

All the nicknames are Americanisms in the broadest sense of that term. Many of the words were coined in America but many others were loan-words, especially from British English, but also from Spanish, French, German, Yiddish, and West African languages—the languages of major immigrant groups. The loanwords became Americanisms, in the broad sense, when they took on new meanings as they were applied, in special circumstances, to groups living in the United States. All the terms are listed in American sources, usually multiple ones, and all are labeled, in at least one source, as having American use.

Excluded are nicknames for residents of many U.S. states, a variety of proposed but never adopted proper names for ethnic groups, terms of general xenophobia used by certain groups for all outgroups, and political epithets referring coincidentally to ethnic groups but without the intent to derogate their ethnicity. Although terms for political and geographic groups are excluded, their close kinship with nicknames for ethnic entities underscores the political and regional dimension of ethnicity in America. Appendix A, near the end of the book, is a short essay on classes of terms that are related to nicknames for specific ethnic groups but are excluded from this list for various reasons.

The conventions of my annotations in the word list are explained in detail in Appendix B, which also includes discussions of problems in etymologies, loanwords, gender referents, devices of pejoration, and other conventions.

The Boundaries of the List. The time span for the accumulation of the words is from the colonial period, when the first terms appeared in American English, to about 1970. Language scholars have not yet recorded, or at least not yet published, nicknames prompted by the newest immigrations, especially since 1965, from Latin America, Asia, and Europe.

As the criterion of inclusion, each word appears in one or more scholarly, published records of slang and dialectal speech in American English. Usually I have listed a term if a scholar reported it, certainly if it is reported with some explanation or if I found it in multiple sources. Many of the terms of course were highly ephemeral, but I have tried to exclude terms that were clearly nonce words.

Many of the terms never had wide, general use in American English, but had restricted use in the slang and dialects of regions, certain cities, social classes, ethnic groups, and other subcultures. I include many words that were local in use, reflecting patterns of ethnic settlement. It cannot be known how widely many words were used, especially the majority that are not familiar today because they have not survived.

All nicknames in the list are to a degree derogatory because they were not the consensually favored name for a group among members of that group. I have made no effort to label the derogation as strong or mild, or as intentional or unintentional. The number of terms for a group indicates the variety of imputed images by which people have tried to diminish the power, cultural authority, or dignity of that group. Almost every American ethnic group with a population exceeding 100,000 has been called recorded nicknames.

Sources. The compilation is secondary in that it is cumulated from published sources. That is, none of the names were collected by my direct observation of use or directly from informants. Most terms have accumulated over many years from edition to edition of certain dictionaries and from generation to generation of dictionaries of Americanisms and slang. Most words for this study were collected by scanning specialized dictionaries and other compilations of Americanisms, which are cited below and listed under References. For the literature before about 1939, I used the dictionaries of Americanisms listed by Burke (1939:2-12).

The nicknames in published sources were compiled by three basic techniques. Early compilations were from observations of everyday speech. Later compilations were collected from the mass media, such as popular and regional novels and newspapers. Most recently, this vocabulary has been collected systematically by sample surveys of local, regional, and national populations (e.g., Pederson 1964; Tarpley 1970; McDavid and Witham 1974; and Cassidy, forthcoming). Most nineteenth-century and earlier terms may be found in De Vere (1871), Bartlett (1877), Maitland (1891), Farmer (1889), Clapin (1902), and Thornton (1912). Many of these terms were brought forward and new twentieth-century words added by Mencken (1936, 1945, 1963), Weseen (1934), Roback (1944), Berrey and Van Den Bark (1953), Weingarten (1954), Franklyn (1963), Major (1970), Roberts (1971), Claerbaut (1972), Dahlskog (1972), Wentworth and Flexner (1975), Spears (1981), and many others. For other than slang, Craigie and Hulbert (1938-44), Mathews (1951), and Avis (1967) were used to date many terms and to identify North Americanisms. For slang, Flexner (1976) is useful for etymologies, for datings, and particularly for setting words in historical contexts. Wall and Przebienda (1969) was used to locate discussions of certain terms in the literature. Partridge (1970) is useful for etymologies of loan words from British English. The several unabridged dictionaries of English were also used for etymologies, though they do not include many terms of slang.

Most nicknames for American ethnic groups have since about 1950 accumulated into a few single sources. About 500 terms appear in Berrey and Van Den Bark (1953), which is the largest single list. Regrettably, they do not include sources, etymologies, or dates for the words. Wentworth and Flexner (1975) list only 275 terms, but supply many datings, etymologies, and examples of literary uses. Spears (1981) lists roughly 600 American terms, collected chiefly from Weseen (1934), Berrey and Van Den Bark (1953), and Wentworth and Flexner (1975).

About one-fourth of the words were collected from other published sources, many of which in other connections are cited in the text. All are scholarly or otherwise reliable records of actual use. Each additional source yielded from one to twenty items. The sources, of course, list many of the same words, though sometimes giving variant meanings, uses, referents, and etymologies. The repetitions and the process of resolving discrepancies served to clarify many issues of group and trait references. As additional items were found less and less often it became clear that closure for this vocabulary was almost complete down to about 1970.

Generic and Particular Terms. All nicknames for ethnic persons are on a continuum from the generic to the particular, from those that refer to any or all persons of a group to those that refer to ethnic persons with a particular trait. Usually, I have included the generic and excluded the highly particular, but I have had to make certain rules about the middle ground. I include all terms that are primarily or exclusively masculine or feminine and all terms that are specific to all children or to all younger or older adults.

Many nicknames originally denominated ethnic persons engaged in socially unapproved roles, such as low-status or stigmatized occupations, military activities against the name-callers, gangsterism, and prostitution. I include all such terms that originally were particular in some way but later became generic or were used with wide, loose application. For example, *hoofer* in the 1920s was a name for a black dancer. The term was generalized to mean other black men; it is included. But *shot*, a black gangster in the same period, apparently was never used more generally; it is excluded. Similarly, *nonpromotable* was a euphemistic term for a black who, simply because of his race, was stuck at a level beneath his qualifications; it is excluded. *Laundry-queen*, on the other hand, apparently was applied widely to black women; it is included.

Finally, some nicknames originally denominated low-status, or less often, high-status segments of a group. These terms are often made generic, and most are included. However, about 500 terms for poor and rustic white Protestants are not included, but in chapter 4 they are separately taken into account.

The Number of Target Groups. The *Harvard Encyclopedia of American Ethnic Groups* (Thernstrom, Orlov, and Handlin 1980) has 106 group entries, which the editors claim are "almost exhaustive" of ethnic groups living in the United States. I found nicknames for 54 groups, all of which correspond to an entry in the *Encyclopedia.* Perhaps as many as 25 additional groups listed in the *Encyclopedia* also have been targets of these terms. Name-callers often do not distinguish, for example, among ethnic groups who speak the same or similar languages, such as Spanish or the Slavic languages. In short, certainly half and perhaps as many as three-quarters of all ethnic groups in the United States have been targets of recorded nicknames. The Armenians, Danes, Finns, and Slovaks are the only sizable European groups for which I found no specific terms. It is also noteworthy that, down to about 1970, I found no words for specific Central or South American groups, Dominicans, or Cubans living in the United States. These groups, nonetheless, were called several of the general terms for any Spanish-speaking person.

Dating. All dates should be considered approximate. Many of the dates, which are taken from highly authoritative sources, are probably accurate to the year indicated. This is usually the date of the earliest example found in print, which does not preclude the existence of yet earlier printed uses and certainly not earlier oral use. My special objective in dating terms is to associate their emergence with historically significant periods, such as wars, economic depressions, migrations, waves of immigration, periods of rapid urbanization, and so on. It is enough for my purposes to fix dates to a decade or even to a wider period. Yet most of the terms are not dated here, for I had no hint from the sources when they appeared. It is particularly difficult to determine when loanwords seeped into American English. Older, better-known terms, especially those considered colloquial or dialectal rather than slang, are more apt to be dated by the sources. Newer, especially slang, terms that appeared in this century are less apt to be dated. Judging from the publication date of the sources, it is my impression that most of the undated terms appeared before 1930, and the vast majority appeared before 1950. Most undated terms in recent dictionaries and word lists can be found in sources published in the 1930s and 1940s. Most nicknames for the European groups who arrived in the "new" immigrations after 1880 had appeared by the 1930s. After about 1930, the elaboration of nicknames for European groups seemed to stabilize while the terms for racial minorities continued to flourish until the 1960s.

The Scheme of Classification. The names are classified by 57 ethnic categories, including several general racial, regional, and religious categories. The terms for each group are listed in alphabetical order under a proper name for the ethnic group. The proper, correct, or preferred name for several groups is at issue. I adopted the proper names used by the *Harvard Encyclopedia of American Ethnic Groups*, though this still leaves several problems.

The largest number of nicknames is aimed at black Americans—over 200 terms and half again as many variants. Terms for blacks and terms for whites used by blacks, the second largest category of terms, are each subclassified by the allusions of the words. (Nicknames for all other groups are, for each group, presented in a single alphabetical list.) For these two longest lists of terms, each aimed at a racial category, it is useful and more readable to subclassify the words. This also shows with two major examples some of the taxonomic problems in developing categories for the examination of stereotypes in the next chapter.

THE WORD LIST

ACADIANS: **acadian-french** [also *acadian-frenchman, french-acadian.* Used for the 20,000 Acadians in northern Maine]; **cajun** [or *cajen.* 1868. Clipped colloquial form of Acadian]; **coon-ass** [also *coonie*]; **cree-owls** [19th century. From a burlesque of *Creole*]; **frenchie, -y; frog** [cf. *frog* for French and French Canadians]; **swamp-rat.**

AFRO-AMERICANS — The Name "Negro" and Its Alterations: **chigro** [a punning blend of *chigg*er and ne*gro*, as a sarcastic allusion to the "proper" name for chiggers, the insects]; **'gar** [clipped form of *niggar,* a dialectal pronunciation of *nigger*]; **negress** [fem. Also *niggeress*]; **negro** [17th century. From Spanish and Portuguese, *negro,* black. On its offensiveness, see Bennett and see Moore]; **negro-fellow** [19th century. Clapin says, "An opprobrious term for a black man, supposed to carry intensive contempt with it"]; **nig** [1828. Shortened from *nigger*]; **nigger** [or *niggor* (1689), *neger, negger*]; **nigger-baby** [a child]; **nigger-boy** [1825]; **niggerdom; nigger-gal** [fem.]; **niggerkin** [a child]; **niggerling** [a child]; **niggero** [a punning blend of *nigger* and *negro*]; **niggra** [or *nigrah.* The infamous mispronunciation of *Negro.* See McDavid (1960) on the pronunciation of *Negro* as a slur]; **nig-nog** [a loanword from British English. Originally, it designated a West Indian or African in the U.K.].

"Black" and Terms Modified by It: **black** [on its offensiveness before the late 1960s, see Robbins]; **blackamoor** [late 17th century. From *black + moor*]; **blackamuffin** [blend of *blackamoor* and *ragamuffin*]; **black-angus; black-bean; black-beauty** [perhaps an allusion either to the novel and movie, *Black Beauty,* about a black horse, or to the 1960s phrase, "black is beautiful"]; **black-bird** [late 19th century]; **black-cunt** [fem.]; **black-diamond; black-doll** [fem.]; **black-fellow** [19th century. Often just *fellow*]; **black-gunga** [origin not known to me]; **black-head; black-indian; black-ivory** [the term for blacks sold in the lucrative African slave trade. Also *black-cattle.* 1819]; **black-jacks; black-mama** [fem.]; **black-out; black-rascal; black-skirt** [fem.]; **black-teapot; black-tulip** [from the popular name for a type of dark-colored tulip]. **blacky, -ey, -ie** [1815].

Color Allusions, Other than "Black" and "Negro": **blue** [19th century.

Also *die Blaue,* which Mencken says was used for black servants by German residents of Baltimore in the 1880s; they changed it to *die Schwarze* when the blacks caught on]; **blue-gum** [1860s]; **blue-skin** [1821. Used by James Fenimore Cooper in *The Spy*]; **brownskin; brownskin-baby** [fem.]; **brown-sugar** [fem. Also *sugar-brown*]; **charcoal; charcoal-blossom** [fem. Also *charcoal-lily*]; **chocolate** [*chokker* and *chokko* are possible variants. Other variants are recent and probably ephemeral college slang. See Dean (1971): *chocolate-bar, chocolate-chip,* etc., and *fudgy, hershey-bar, tootsie-roll,* etc.]; **chocolate-drop** [fem. 1912]; **club** [cf. *ace-of-spades, spade*]; **coal** [fem.]; **coal-shutes-blackie; colored** [1820s. Also *the-colored, cullud, the-cullud, cullud-gemman,* and *colored-folk, -people, -person, -boy, -man.* Also, in 1796, *people-of-color, person-, woman-, man-*]; **crow** [1730s. See Dillard (1977: 68, 164) on *Jim Crow*]; **cullud-gal** [fem.]; **dark-brethern; dark-cloud** [1900. Also used for any gathering of blacks]; **dark-meat** [fem. Also *black-meat, piece-of-dark-meat, rare-peice-of-dark-meat, hot-piece-of-dark-meat*]; **darky, -ee, -ey, ie** [1775]; **domino; dusky, dusky-dame** [fem.]; **ebony** [1850s. Also, rarely, *a-little-bit-of-ebony, God's-image-cut-in-ebony,* etc.]; **eightball** [1931. An allusion to the black color of the pool ball]; **femmoke** [probably from *fem* or *femme,* slang term for a woman, and *moke.* Cf. *moke*]; **gelbe** [from *die Gelbe,* the yellows. Mencken (1944) reports Jewish use in New York City. Cf. *blue* and *schwarze*]; **hot-chocolate** [fem. Also *sweet-chocolate.* Cf.*chocolate-drop*]; **indian-princess** [fem. A jocular euphemism]; **ink** [also *ink-face, ink-spitter, inky-dink*]; **jaybee** [an initialism, *j.b.,* for *jet black*]; **licorice** [also *licorice-stick*]; **lily-white** [a deliberate paradox]; **load-of-coal** [used for any gathering of blacks. Cf.*dark-cloud*]; **mocha** [often fem. Probably from *mocha,* the color and the blend of coffee and chocolate. Used as an adjective since the 1850s. Cf. *moke*]; **moke** [1856. Probably a clipping of *smoke,* but possibly from *mocha.* Cf. Toll (pp. 132-33), Flexner (1976), and Mencken (1944)]; **molonjohn** [used by Italians. Probably from Italian *melanzana,* eggplant. Also *eggplant*]; **painted-goof; pink-tongue** [also *white-palms,* etc.]; **raisin** [perhaps from the play and 1961 movie *Raisin in the Sun*]; **raven-beauty** [fem. A pun]; **redbone** [fem.]; **schocherer** [19th century. Jewish use. Appel says "a fairly exact transliteration of the Hebrew word for 'black,' with the suffix *-er* appended"]; **schwarze** [or *schwarz, swatzy, schwerze, swartzy, schvartza,* *schvartze, schvartzeh, schwartze, schvartzer, schwartzer*. Mainly, Jewish and German use, eventually passing into American slang]; **scuttle** [from "coal-scuttle." Also *hod*, another word for "coal scuttle"]; **scuttle-sault** [fem. Origin of *sault* is unclear to me. Perhaps from an old word for a woman, as an instance of sexual intercourse; it is also a variant spelling of *salt*. Cf. *pale-sault* for a white woman]; **seal** [often fem. 1930]; **shade** [1960s]; **shadow** [cf. *shade*]; **shady-lady** [fem. A pun on *shade*]; **skillet** [1930s]; **smidget; smoke** [1920s. Also *smokey, -y*, and *smokey-joe*]; **smoked-irishman; smoked-yankee** [1820s. A freed black]; **smudge; smutt-butt; snowball** [1780. A deliberate paradox. Cf. *lily-white*. Recent variants are *snow-cone, snow-flake*]; **snuff** [perhaps from the color of snuff or using snuff]; **spade** [1919. From, and also, *ace-of-spades*]; **spaginzy** [1950s. Perhaps related to *spade*, altered to *spag*. Note that formed like *ofaginzy*, a black term for whites]; **stove-lid; suede** [presumably from the often dark color of suede]; **sunburned-irishman; tar-baby** [often *nigger-tar-baby*. Also *tar-pot*. All mean a child]; **tarbrushed-folk; tar-heel** [probably an extension of *Tar Heel*, the nickname for a North Carolinian]; **tar-pot** [a child]; **unbleached-american** [late 19th century].

Allusions to Other Physical Differences: **bootlips; brillo-head** [from the brand name of the steel-wool scouring pad. Also *wire-head, curly-head*]; **broad-nose; buffalo** [perhaps from *buffalo-soldier* (1873), a black soldier so called on the American frontier because their hair texture was thought to resemble the coat of the buffalo]; **burr-head** [also *burry-head*]; **fuzzy; kinky** [1844. Also *kink, kinky-head, kinky-nob*]; **long-heels; moss; nappy** [also *nap*]; **saucer-lips** [especially, fem. Also *ubangi*]; **thicklips; wooly-head** [1827. First found in James Fenimore Cooper's *The Prairie*. Also *wool*].

Given Personal Names: **aunt-jemima** [fem. Popularized by a minstrel song, "Old Aunt Jemima," 1876-77, and later reinforced by the "Aunt Jemima" brand of pancake mix]; **cuffee, -y** [1713, down to 1880s. Also *cuff. Cuddy* seems to be a later alteration. From the West African day name, *Cuffee, -y*, for a male child born on Friday. See Dillard (p. 91) on the African day names]; **george; james; juba; leroy; liza** [fem. Late 19th century. Also *lize*]; **mandy** [fem.]; **mose** [from *Moses*]; **quashee, -ie, -ey** [1840s. From the West African day name, *Quashee*, Ashanti for a male child born on Sunday. Also *squasho* (1900)]; **rastus** [popular by 1896];

sambo [or *zambo*. 1806. From either American Spanish *zambo*, a black or mulatto, or a Hausan word meaning "second son"]; **sapphire** [fem. Perhaps from the character on the *Amos and Andy* show]; **willie, -y.**

Personality and Group Character: **buggy** [from the slang term, *buggy*, crazy. Probably reinforced by *boogie*. Sometimes euphemized to *buggy-whip*]; **drum** [from, according to Landy, the name of a fictional character]; **hand-jiver** [also *finger-popper*]; **lightening** [cf. *brer-terrapin*]; **mister-honest; moon-doggie** [origin not known to me]; **nigger-trigger** [also *nigger-shooter*]; **night-creeper** [also *nightowl, midnighter*]; **night-fighter** [also *alabama-night-fighter*]; **russian** [1942. From a pun on *rushing*, as in "rushin' away from hard work," "rushin' up North," etc.]; **spook** [1940. Also *spook-cat*]; **sunshine** [also *summertime*].

Occupational Stereotypes: **boots** [from a nickname for a shoe-shine man in a hotel or train station. Also *shoe-shine* and *shoe-shine-boy*]; **cotton-picker; field-hand** [19th century or earlier. Also *field-nigger*]; **hoofer** [1925. From the reputation of originating and popularizing dances on the vaudeville stage. Also *tap-dancer*]; **junk-man; laundry-queen** [fem.]; **mammy** [also *maumer*. 19th century or earlier. Also *nigger-mammy*]; **shine** [1902. Origin not known to me. Perhaps shortened from *shoe-shine*, a variant of *boots*. Possible variant is *shin(n)y* (1893). Irwin says "from the sweaty, shiny appearance of the skin." But see De Vere].

Allusions to African Origins: **afric; african** [early 18th century]; **african-reject** [*african-runner*, etc.]; **afro; congo** [1760]; **ethiopian** [19th century]; **guinea** [1789. Also *guinea-negro* (19th century)]; **hottentot; ibo** [1732. Thornton, volume 3, says *ebo* was used in 1822 and speculates that it is from *ebony*. But *ebony* for a black was first used in the 1850s. Dalby says *ebo* is a variant of *ibo*]; **mollygasher** [19th century. Probably an alteration of *Malagasy*, i.e., a black thought to be from Madagascar]; **nigerian** [ostensibly from *Nigerian* but serves as a euphemism for *nigger*]; **senegambian** [1888]; **spear-chucker; zulu** [1920s. Also *zoolo*].

Other Cultural Allusions: **all-god's-chillun(s); alligator-bait** [also clipped to *'gator-bait*. Usually a child]; **black-silk-socks** [from a type of hosiery favored by older black men]; **boogie, -y** [1920s. Probably an alteration of *booger* ("bogeyman"). Also *bo, bu, boog, booger, boo-boo*]; **buckwheat** [perhaps from an historical association of blacks with eating of buckwheat; possibly influenced by the name of "Buckwheat" Thomas, the black actor in the "Our Gang" movie series]; **cantaloupe** [chiefly used by Italians. Origin not known to me]; **conch** [from the name of the gastropod. A 19th-century name for Bahamians, which by the 1920s was applied to West Indians in the U.S.]; **contraband** [1861, down to about 1900. Also *intelligent-contraband*. From a U.S. proclamation issued in 1861 declaring slaves owned by Confederates a "contraband" of war]; **exoduster** [1880. Weingarten says "A Negro who left the South to settle in the North at the time of the Exodus"]; **free-issue** [after 1865. A term for a free-born black. This is one of several Reconstruction terms, such as *fifteenth-amendment-persuasion*, *f.m.c.*, as initialism for *free man of color*, and *freedman*. Cf. *free-jack*]; **free-jack** [late 19th century. A freed slave. Later shortened to *jack* and used for any black]; **gange, -y** [or *kange*, *-y*. Origin not known to me]; **geech** [shortened from *Geechee*, a Gullah-speaking black in South Carolina]; **harlemaniac** [from blend of *Harlem* and *maniac*. A related sentiment is in *ghetto-ghoul*]; **highpockets** [also *short-coat*]; **jazzbo** [19th century. Uncertain origin]; **jig(g)** [1923. Shortened from *jigaboo*. Also *jiga*, *jigger*, *nig-a-jig*, *zig*]; **jigabo(o)** [1910. *Jig + aboo*, as in *bugaboo*. Also *jibagoo* (an inversion of *jigaboo*), *jiggerboo*, *zig(g)abo(o)*. Uncertain origin. See Flexner (1976) for possibilities]; **jim-crow** [Flexner (1976) says it was introduced by Thomas D. Rice's 1828 minstrel song "Jim Crow." Popular in 1880s and 1890s. Cf. *crow*]; **marcus** [also *garvey*. From the name of Marcus Garvey, 1887-1940, the black leader]; **mayate** [or *mayata*. From Chicano Spanish *mayate*, a U.S. black person]; **monkey-chaser** [1920s. Originally a West Indian]; **peanut** [perhaps from an association with George Washington Carver. But a *peanut* is also a person of small value. Cf. *jit*, *dink*, etc.]; **pickaninny** [or *piccaninny*. 1800. Also shortened to *'ninny* and altered to *pickney*. From Portuguese *pequenino*, little one, through Pidgin English]; **rights** [1960s. Sometimes punned to *riots*. The Civil Rights movement, like the Reconstruction a century earlier, spawned a host of short-lived nicknames, such as *brother-of-america*, *sister-woman*, *soul-leg*, *token-nigger*, and other sarcastic associations with symbols of the period]; **scram; splib** [a black term. Origin not known to me. Sometimes used by whites and, when so, is derogatory and offensive]; **tutsoon** [chiefly used by Italians. Possibly from an Italian word, but I cannot hear it in the alteration]; **uncle-remus** [inspired by Uncle Remus of the Joel Chandler Harris stories].

Animal Metaphors: **ape** [also *baboon*]; **bat** [fem.]; **brer-terrapin** [also *terrapin*]; **buck** [1800. Also *buck-nigger* (1842)]; **bull-nigger** [19th century]; **coon** [1862. Popular after 1896. From *raccoon*. See discussion in chapter 1]; **crow** [1730s]; **jar-head** [the same term, a Southernism, means a mule]; **jungle-bunny** [1920s. Also *african-bunny, nairobi-jackrabbit*]; **mare-nigger** [fem.]; **monkey; monkey-jane** [fem. 1920s]; **mule; muskrat** [also shortened to *musk*]; **possum** [from *opossum*, supposedly either for hunting or for eating them]; **skunk** [often *black-skunk*].

Stereotypes of Low Intelligence: **hard-head** [also *thick-head, bone-head*]; **rock** [perhaps shortened from such as "rock-head"].

Status Diminution: **aunt** [fem. Early 1830s. Also *auntie, -ey*. Used for older women]; **bad-nigger** [19th century]; **bitch;** [fem. Often *black-bitch*]; **boy** [1630s. Often *black-boy*]; **covess-dinge** [fem. 1850s. *Covess,* a woman, from *cove,* old slang for a fellow. Cf. *dinge*]; **dange-broad** [fem. From old adjective *dange,* sexy]; **dinge** [1848. Backformation from *dingey, -y* (1909), often a child]; **dink** [perhaps a backformation from *dinky* (adj.), of small value. Also *dinkey* for a child (late 19th century)]; **goon** [perhaps shortened from *gooney,* a simpleton. *Goonie,* for a black U.S. Virgin Islander, is a possible cognate]; **jit** [especially, fem. From *jitney,* a five-cent piece, hence a thing of small value]; **poontang** [fem. 1870s. From Louisiana French *putain,* whore]; **pork-chop** [a term applied also to other groups]; **seedy; trash** [often *black-trash*]; **uncle** [late 1820s. Used for older men. Cf. *aunt, auntie*]; **wench** [fem. 1765. Often *negro-* or *nigger-wench* (1715)].

AMERICAN INDIANS: **abergoin** [or *abrogan.* 19th century. Alterations of *aborigine*]; **barbarian** [19th century. Also *heathen, beast, wildman.* Cf. *savage* and *siwash*]; **blanket-indian** [1875. Also *stick-indian* and other terms for unassimilated Indians]; **bow-and-arrow** [also *war-whoop* and other such images]; **brave** [1837. Used by James Fenimore Cooper. From French, *brave,* brave, good, worthy]; **buck** [1630]; **chief** [also *chief-rain-in-the-face, sitting-bull,* and other sarcastic applications of the idea of "chief"]; **copperhead** [used by early Dutch settlers. From the name of the snake to connote color and treachery]; **hiawatha** [from the namesake character in "The Song of Hiawatha," an 1855 verse by Longfellow]; **hooch** [or *hootch.* 1899. Probably from the reputation of high alcohol consumption by some Natives. *Hooch,* meaning liquor, is short for

Hoochinoo, an alteration of *Hutsnuwu*, the name of an Alaskan Indian group who made liquor]; **injun** [1825. Colloquial for *Indian* (1602). Earlier form was *injen* (1680)]; **'jin** [1940s. Used by blacks. A clipped and altered *injun*]; **lo** [also *mister-lo* (1871), *poor-lo* (1891). Mencken (1963) says derived from Alexander Pope's verse: "Lo, the poor Indian! whose untutor'd mind / Sees God in clouds, or hears him in the wind"]; **mister-john** [1870]; **papoose** [1633. From Algonquian for "baby" or "child." Later used for any Native child]; **red** [1878]; **red-brother** [1832]; **red-devil** [1834]; **red-indian** [1878]; **red-man** [1725]; **red-race** [19th century]; **red-skin** [1699]; **savage** [late 19th century. Cf. *siwash*]; **siwash** [1852. Also *siwash-indian*. From French *sauvage*, savage]; **smoked-ham; smokey, son-of-the-forest; squaw** [1634. From various Algonquian words for "woman." Later used for any Native woman]; **vanishing-american.**

NOTE: Many nicknames for specific ethnic groups and local settlements of Native American Indians, which were used locally, are omitted from this list. The list is confined to nicknames that were used for any Indian, regardless of ethnicity.

APPALACHIANS: **briar; brush-ape** [1920]; **corn-cracker** [19th century]; **hard-head; hillbilly** [c. 1900. The *-billy* component is a nickname for any fellow]; **hillnelly** [fem. Modeled on *hillbilly*]; **mountain-boomer** [also *mountain-hoosier*]; **mountaineer; mountie; one-eye** [Wentworth and Flexner say that the term is from a belief that inbreeding in isolated hill communities cause eyes, through successive generations, to become closer together]; **ridge-runner; sam** [acronym for Southern Appalachian migrant]; **snake** [originally a West Virginian]; **wasp** [1950s. The acronym for White Appalachian Southern Protestant. Used for migrants to Chicago and other midwestern industrial cities].

ARABS; **aye-rab** [a deliberate mispronunciation of *Arab*, and it is offensive. See Lipski. Cf. *eye-talian* for Italians]; **dirty-arab; sheik** [especially offensive when pronounced "sheek"].

AUSTRALIANS AND NEW ZEALANDERS: **aussie, -ey** [or *ossie, ozzie*. Popular since WWI. Variantly, *arsie, -ey*, whose pejoration or jocularity is possibly reinforced by sound similarity to *arse*. All are short for *Australian*]; **cornstalk** [Partridge says from tall, slim physical appearance]; **currency-lad** [late 19th century. Perhaps, I speculate, a version of "remittance man," a soft, middle-class and unsuccessful Englishman in Australia who is dependent on "remittances" or on money from home]; **digger** [WWI. From an old Australianism and the popular name for Australian and New Zealander soldiers]; **kiwi; orsetralian** [a mimicking of an Australian pronunciation of *Australian*. Also *'strine*]; **pome** [origin uncertain. Legendarily, an acronym for *Prisoner of Mother England*. A less fanciful possible origin is from *pome*granate, as an allusion to the sunburned skin of fair immigrants. Cf. *redneck* for Southerners. Apparently, a transference of *pommy*, a term for Englishmen in Australia. See Partridge (1970)]; **sooner** [probably from a slang term for a sponger or one who will do anything "sooner" than work for a living].

BASQUES: **basco** [originally a sheepherder].

BELGIANS: **belgeek** [a phonetic spelling of French *Belgique*, Belgium]; **belgie; blemish** [probably an altered blend of *Belg*ian and Fle*mish*, perhaps also reinforced by negative connotations of *blemish*]; **flamingo** [early 20th century. Partridge says from sound of French *Flamand*, Flemish, as if "flaming." French *flamant* means "flamingo." The words *flamingo*, the bird, *flame*, the color of the bird, and *Fleming*, the nationality, are etymologically related].

BULGARIANS: **burglar** [apparently only from slight similarity of spelling]; **vulgarian.**

CANADIANS, BRITISH: **anglo** [1800. Also *anglo-saxon*]; **anglo-bluenose** [1845. Particularly a Maritimer but, loosely, any Anglo-Canadian]; **bingboy** [I speculate from *bingo-boy*, a drunk]; **english** [used derogatorily for Scots and Irish Canadians by French Canadians, implying their assimilation to English ways. Also *englishman, english-canadian*]; **qwasp** [an acronym for Quebec White Anglo-Saxon Protestants]; **tom** [late 1960s. Acronym for a national elite, predominantly Anglophones, who, it is thought, concentrate in Toronto, Ottawa, and Montreal. See Colombo (1979). Possibly also alludes to *tom* or *tommy* for the British English].

NOTE: Several nicknames for Anglo-Canadians are specific to residents of particular provinces, especially the Maritime Provinces, such as *blue-nose* [1830], *herring-choker, newf* [also *newfie, newfier*], and *novy*. These terms are excluded from the above list and the tabulation for the same reasons (see Appendix A) that nicknames for residents of particular states in the United States are excluded.

CATHOLICS (generic terms): **beadpuller** [also *bead-counter*. An allusion to use of the rosary]; **cat-lick** [also shortened to *lick*. Word plays on *Catholic*. Perhaps reinforced by old spelling, Cath*olick*]; **crawthumper** [1845. Also altered to *claw-thumper*. In U.S., directed at early Catholic settlers in Maryland. Grose in 1785 listed *craw-thumper* as a generic term for Catholics, "from their beating their breasts in the confession of their sins." Variant *chest-pounder* is an Americanism for any Catholic]; **crossback** [origin not known to me. Perhaps, I speculate, from design on priest's vestment or chasuble]; **fish-eater** [also *guppy-gobbler*]; **mackerel-snapper** [also *mackerel-snatcher*]; **papist** [also shortened to *pape*]; **poper; r.c.; right-foot** [also *right-hander*. Cf. *left-foot* and *left-hander* as generic terms for Protestants]; **roman** [from "*Roman* Catholic Church"]; **statue-lover** [also *statue-worshiper*]; **turk** [perhaps a generalization from *turk* for the Irish Catholics. In the 19th century, Catholics also were generically called *micks*].

CHINESE: **almond-eye** [used also for other Asians]; **buddha-head** [used also for other Asians]; **celestian** [or *celestial*. 1843. From the name "Celestial Empire," the former Chinese Empire]; **charlie** [used also for other Asians]; **china-boy; chinaman** [1849. Also *chinamang*, where final "g" may mimic a sound in Chinese speech]; **chinawoman** [fem. 1872]; **chinee** [1870. Also *heathen-chinee*. Probably from Bret Harte's verse "Truthful Jones"]; **ching-doll** [fem.]; **chink** [1880. Also *chinky* (1880), *chinky-chinky-chinaman*]; **chino; chow** [also *chow-mein*. From Cantonese *cha'ao*, fry]; **coolie** [19th century. Originally any Oriental laborer. From Hindi, *kuli*, laborer]; **coosie** [1943]; **flange-head** [WWII]; **john** [also *johnny, john-* or *johnny-chinaman*. All 1852-53]; **li'l-eyes** [used also for other Asians]; **little-brown-brother** [WWII]; **ming** [also pidgin *mink*]; **mochalie** [perhaps a diminutive of *mocha*, as color reference]; **monk** [before 1925. Also *monkey*]; **moon-eyed-leper; mustard; pigtail; pong** [perhaps from "ong" sound in some Chinese speech]; **rice-belly; rice-man** [mainly black use]; **segoonya** [fem. Origin not known to me]; **slant** [short for *slant-eye*. Also used for other Asians]; **slope** [short for *slope-head*]; **slopie** [WWII]; **slopie-gal** [fem.]; **squint-eyes; yellow-bastard; yellow-belly** [used also for other Asians]; **yellow-fish** [specifically an illegal immigrant in U.S. *To-move-the-laundry* meant to smuggle Chinese]; **yellow-man** [also *yellow-boy*]; **yellow-peril** [also *yellow-horde*. Used also for other Asian groups].

CORNISH: **cousin-jack** [also *cousin-jacky, cousin-jan. Cousin* was used for any distant kinsman. Note that *cousin-jack* was also used for the Welsh in the U.S.]; **cousin-jenny** [fem.].

CZECHS: **bohunk** [1890s. Most common 1900-35. Also *bohak, bohick, bohink,* and *bohve.* A blend of Bohemian and Hungarian. The *-hung* component is probably reinforced by *hunk*]; **bootchkey** [or *butchski, butski.* Roback says from *počkej,* "hold on," a children's cry]; **bujak** [used also for other Slavic groups. Origin not known to me]; **check** [also *zek.* Both alterations of *Czech*]; **chesky, -ey** [1926. From *czezski*]; **chessie** [apparently an alteration of *Czech*]; **duke** [a general term used for several groups]; **honyock** [a rustic Czech in Nebraska]; **hunk** [1896. Also *hunky* (1900). Also for Hungarians and other Central European groups]; **mushroom-picker** [probably from the popular recreation in Central European countries].

DUTCH: **black-dutch;** **butter-mouth** [also *butter-box*]; **cabbage-head** [1854. Cf. same word for Germans. *Cabbage-head* was 1890s slang for a stupid person]; **closh** [from *Claus,* a nickname for *Nicholas.* Also *mynheer-closh*]; **copperhead** [19th century. Specifically the Dutch in New York]; **dutcher** [also *dutchie.* Cf. same words used for Germans, as alterations of *Deutsch,* German]; **frank** [1848]; **froglander; hans; jankaas** [17th century. See etymology of *yankee* under YANKEES]; **knickerbocker** [1831. Generalized to all descendants of New York Dutch]; **nicfrog** [*nic-* is probably from *Nic* or *Nick,* short for *Nicholas*]; **pickleherring; wooden-shoe.**

EAST INDIANS: **rag-head** [1920s. Also *towel-head, diaper-head*]; **wog** [etymology is uncertain. Perhaps from *golliwog(g),* a grotesque black doll or a grotesque person. Certainly *wog* is not an acronym for *wily* (or *wonderful*) oriental gentleman. See Spears for another hypothesis].

ENGLISH: **beef-eater** [20th century. Probably from fame of English roast beef, reinforced by "Beefeater," as a Warder of the Tower of London. Earlier, in Britain, a "beefeater" or a "loafeater" was a well-fed menial who earned his board and keep]; **bimshah** [in U.S., it has been a black term for an Englishman. I speculate it is a variant of *bimshire,* which in the 19th century was a West Indian name for a resident of Barbados, which was called "Little England." Perhaps reinforced by English slang, *bim,* a thinning of *bum,* posterior]; **briton** [18th century. Thornton says "somewhat offensively applied to Englishmen in Connecticut"]; **brit-tisher** [19th century or earlier. Thornton says "derogatory"]; **bug** [18th century. Originally Irish usage, from bugs introduced into Ireland, Irish folklore has it, by the English]; **bull-lion** [1877]; **chirper** [1912. Also *sparrow*. Both by association with the "English sparrow" and used especially for a Cockney]; **cockney** [when applied to all English people]; **corkney** [cf. *cockney*. A double pun on Cockney accent and alleged Cockney drinking habits]; **englisher** [1843]; **godam** [or *goddam*. From French slang, mocking the English curse]; **islander; joan-bull** [fem. Variant of *john-bull*]; **john-bull** [also *johnny-bull*. From the principal character, John Bull, in Arbuthnot's 1712 allegory, *The History of John Bull*]; **johnny, -ie; lime-juicer** [1880s. From the lime juice historically served on British ships. Also *lime-juice, lemon-eater, lemon-sucker*]; **limey** [1910. From *lime-juicer*]; **roineck** [a loan from Afrikaans *rooinek*, redneck, used for Englishmen in the Boer War]; **tommy** [WWII. Probably a shortening of *Tommy* Atkins, any private in the British army, parallel to G.I. *Joe* in America]; **wasc** [acronym for white Anglo-Saxon Catholic. Used for English Catholic settlements in U.S.].

ESKIMOS: **eskimo-indian** [1742]; **esky, -ie** [short for *Eskimo*]; **esquaw** [fem. Possibly from a variant of Algonquian *squa*, woman, hence *squaw* or perhaps a blend of Eskimo and *squaw*]; **esquimuff** [fem. Perhaps from an alteration of *Esquimau* or possibly a blend of *Esquimau* and *muff*, which has been a slang term for a woman, the female pubes, and a stupid person, and is the name of a fur-mitten]; **husky** [1830. Probably an abbreviation of some early variant of *Eskimo*, perhaps *eskie, -ey*. This is also the origin of the name of the sled dog, which today might reinforce *husky* as a derogatory allusion. The name *Eskimo* itself was originally an Indian epithet for an Innuit, meaning "eater of raw meat," and derives from Algonquian, probably through Canadian French *Esquimau*]; **squaw** [fem. A misnomer. Cf. *eskimo-indian*]; **'skimo** [or *skimau*. 1837. Also *'skim*]; **suchemo** [or *suckemo*. 1852. Also *seymo*. Alterations of *Eskimo*].

FILIPINOS: **brown-brother; brownie; chico** [probably from Spanish *chico*, boy. This may recall former Philippine associations with Spain. Rarely, Filipinos also were called *spick*]; **filipinyock** [perhaps a blend from *Fili-pin*(o) + *yock*, the latter element being, says Franklyn, American-Yiddish slang, *yock*, a back-slang rendering of *goy*. But, notes Franklyn, *hon-*

yock(er) is a pejorative term for a poor white or rustic]; **fip** [also *flip*. Probably altered short forms of *Filipino*]; **goo-goo** [or *gu-gu*. 1925. Originally a Filipino soldier in the Spanish-American War, 1899-1902. Perhaps a mimicry of speech sounds, and other possibilities. See Flexner (1976)]; **gook** [origin unknown. Used also for other Pacific groups]; **philip** [probably short for *Philippine*, which was named after King Philip II of Spain]; **phillipean** [or *philipeen*. Fem. Certainly influenced by sound and spelling similarity to *Philippine* and *Filipino*. But, I conjecture, it is also from the unrelated *philopena*, *fillipeen*, *phillipina*, etc., which are all altered, Anglicized forms of German *Vielliebchen*, darling, sweetheart].

NOTE: All nicknames for Filipinos originated outside the United States as a result of the Spanish-American War, American colonialism in the Philippines, and World War II.

FRENCH: **dee-donk** [or *didonk*. WWI. Probably from sound of *dis donc*, "Hey, tell me"]; **frencher** [1826. Perhaps from use in Cooper's *The Last of the Mohicans*. Also *frenchy*, *-ie* (1883)]; **frog** [also *froggy*, *-ie*. WWI. Sometimes pig-Latin *ogfray*, frog. Sometimes *tadpole* for a child. Also *frog-eater* (1850) and *frog-legs* (fem.). Also *crapaud*, *jean-crapaud*, *johnny-crapaud*. Also altered to *crappo*, *crow-poo*. All from French *crapaud*, toad, dialectally "frog"]; **jean** [also *johnny*]; **jean-potage; mounseer** [also *mosoo* or *mossoo*. From French *monsieur*, mister]; **parleyvoo** [1891. From French, *parlez-vous*].

FRENCH-CANADIANS: **canuck** [or *canack*, *canuk*, *cunnuck*, *kanuck*, *k'nuck,*, etc. 1855. Probably from Hawaiian *kanacka*, man, by way of French *canaque*. See chapter 6. Also *johnny-canuck*]; **canajun** [perhaps a blend of *Cana*dian and cad*jun* or in*jun*]; **french-fries** [also *frit*. Probably from French *frites*, fried potatoes, i.e., "French fries"]; **frenchy, -ie** [1891. Also *frenchman* (1856)]; **frog** [also *froggy*, *-ie*, *ogfray* (pig-Latin for *frog*), *frog-eater* (1923). Also *crapaud*, *johnny-crapaud* (from French *crapaud*, toad, dialectally "frog")]; **jean-baptiste** [also *jean-batiste*, *john-baptiste* (1818). Also *jean-courteau* (1901)]; **joe; johnny-cake** [Roback says from phrase in Montreal children's doggerel c. 1900: "French peasoup and johnnycake / Make your father a bellyache"]; **johnny-peasoup** [1896. Also *french-peasoup*, *peasoup*, and *peasouper*]; **pepsi** [from an alleged predilection for Pepsi-Cola]; **quebecker** [1836].

GERMANS: boche [or *bosche.* Also *alboche.* WWI. From *alboche,* a contraction of French Al(lemand) + (ca)*boche,* roughly, German "blockhead"]; bucket-head [WWI]; busher [also *bushe.* Perhaps a variant of *boche.* Yet, note that Irwin said *busher* was hobo slang for an outsider]; cabbage-head [1854. Cf. same word for Dutch. *Cabbage-head* was 1890s slang for a stupid person]; cousin-michael [from *der deutsche Michel,* the German peasantry]; dummerhead [19th century. From German *dummkopf,* blockhead, simpleton]; dutch [1742. Also *dutcher, dutchman* (1778), *dutchy, -ie*]; fräulein [fem.]; fritz [WWI. Also *fritzie. -y*]; goon [WWI]; gretchen [fem.]; hans [late 19th century, but popular after WWI and WWII]; hans-wurst [also *wurst*]; heinie, -ey [1904. From diminutive of *Heinrich*]; hitlander [WWII]; hohenzollern [from the name of the former royal family of Germany]; honyock [specifically a rustic German in Nebraska]; hop-head [probably an allusion to hops in German beer]; hun [1908]; iroquois-of-europe; jerry [or *gerry.* WWI. From either the English slang term for a chamber pot or the first syllable in *German*]; johnny-squarehead [also *squarehead* (WWII)]; kamerad [WWI. From German *Kamerad,* mate, and a supposed call of surrendering German soldiers]; limburger [1904. Or *limberger.* Also *limberg*]; metzel [perhaps from the German American dish metzel-soup]; nazi [WWII. As applied to German-Americans]; pretzel; prussian [as an allusion to military aggressiveness]; rhinelander; sauerkraut [or *-krout.* 1904. Also *kraut* (WWI), *krauthead* (WWII)]; sausage [1880s]; turner [19th century. From Turnverein, the popular athletic or gymnastic societies of German Americans]; vaterländer.

GREEKS: asshole-bandit [from popular stories about buggery]; greaseball [a term for several groups but applied specifically to Greeks]; grikola [Pederson (1964) speculates term to be from school-boy Latin *agricola,* farmer]; johnny [a term for several groups but applied specifically to Greeks]; marble-head [19th century. Perhaps from popular imagery of the marble statuary of ancient Greece. Cf. *buddha-head* for the Chinese].

GYPSIES: bohemian [19th century]; bush-cove [19th century. Partridge (1970) repeats, "from their lodging under the hedges, etc." *Cove* is an old word for "fellow"]; fair-gang [19th century. Partridge (1970) says from frequenting country fairs in groups. Or, he adds, "Probably a corruption of *faw-gang*, itself *ex Faa*, a Scottish-Gypsy surname"]; **gyp** [or *gip, jip*. 19th century. Also *gipper, gippo, jippo*]; **moon-man** [19th century. Perhaps influenced by an identical old slang term for a robber by night]; **pikey** [19th century. Partridge suggests it is related to *pike* and *piker*, a footlose person on the old turnstile roads, i.e., a tramp. Cf. *pike*, a 19th-century term for a U.S. Southerner who was a migrant to California].

HUNGARIANS: **bohunk** [1890s. A blend of *Bo*hemian and *Hung*arian. Sometimes thinned to *bohink*. By 1903, used for any East or Central European group]; **goulash; horwat** [1919. Probably from a surname]; **hun** [from a shortening of *Hungarian*]; **hungry** [apparently a pun on *Hungary*]; **hunk** [1896. Also *hunky, -ie* (1900), *hunky-chunk*].

ICELANDERS: **goolie** [origin unknown].

IRISH: **bark** [1840s. Origin not known to me]; **baytzimer** [or *betzemer, batesomer*. Occurs only in this plural form. Also *mishter-behtzimer*. From Hebrew *bezim*, eggs. Used in 1890s by Jews in New York City. Perhaps influenced by the similarity of sound of German *Irlander*, Irishman, and *eirer*, eggs. See Appel, Glanz (1966). *Baitsim*, probably the same word, is American Yiddish slang for testicles]; **bogger; bog-lander** [18th century]; **bog-rat; bog-trotter** [1848. Also *bog-hopper*]; **boiled-dinner; bridget** [fem. Also diminutive *biddy* (1870)]; **brogueneer; chaw** [also *chew-mouth*. Probably from slang *chaw*, a yokel. Perhaps influenced by meaning of *chaw* as rude, noisy eating]; **croppie** [origin not known to me]; **dogan** [probably from a surname]; **donovan; emeralder** [1845. From the "Emerald Isle"]; **fighting-irish** [1830]; **flamed-mouth** [origin not known to me]; **flannel-mouth** [1870. An allusion either to blarney or to thickness of speech from a brogue or from drink]; **girleen** [fem. Diminutive of *girl*]; **greek** [1848. Also, especially for an immigrant, *grecian*]; **greenhorn** [also used for other immigrant groups]; **harp** [1900. Most common c.1925. Also *harpy*. Probably from the national symbol]; **hibernian** [1830]; **irisher** [1807]; **mac** [from prefix of many Irish surnames. Cf. *mack* for Scots]; **michael; mick** [1856. Also *mickey, -y*. From *Michael*]; **mike** from *Michael*]; **mulligan; murphy** [also *murph* and, phonetically, *moiphy*. 19th century]; **paddy** [1852. From *Padraig*, Gaelic form of *Patrick*]; **paddywhack** [or *paddy-wack*. An allusion to loss of temper and fighting]; **pat** [1830. Short for, and also, *patrick* (1841). Also *patty*]; **patess** [fem.]; **patlander** [1839. Also *paddylander*]; **peat-bogger; peat-digger; potato-eater** [also *potato-head*, etc.]; **redshanks** [originally a Celtic native of Ireland. From an allusion to color of bare legs reddened by exposure]; **ruddy-duck** [perhaps because this species of North American duck is colloquially called a *paddywhack* or *paddy*]; **saltwater-turkey** [an immigrant Irishman who has "crossed the saltwater." See *turkey*]; **shamrock** [also shortened to *sham*]; **shanty-irish** [1925. Also *cheap-shanty-mick*]; **shoneen** [from Irish Gaelic *Seoinīn*, diminutive of *Seon*, John. Originally an upstart]; **son-of-erin**; **spud** [cf. *potato-eater*]; **surly-boy**; **tad** [1904. Diminutive of *Thaddeus*]; **teague**; **teddy** [1900. Also *ted*. Both diminutives of *Theodore*]; **terrier** [perhaps jocular to suggest an Irish terrier dog. *Terrier* or *tarrier* was 1890s slang for a tough man, a loafer]; **turf-cutter**; **turk** [1914. Probably from Gaelic *torc*, boar, pig. See McLaughlin. Cf. *turkey*]; **turkey** [see McCarthy]; **whiskey-mick**; **wog** [apparently another American extension of the Britishism, as Americans use *wog* for the Vietnamese].

ITALIANS: **antonio; banana-peddler; carlo; dago** [since 1858. From Spanish *Diego*, James]; **dingbat** [also rarely for Chinese. Origin unknown]; **dino** [probably diminutive for *Constantino*]; **duke** [cf. *wop*]; **eyetalian** [1840. Weingarten says, "a written form of Italian, used slightingly." It is also a deliberate mispronunciation and it is offensive. See Lipski]; **eyetie** [or *eytie, -ity, -itey*. Early 20th century]; **gangster** [also *hoodlum*]; **gi-gi** [Mencken (1963) says used in Louisiana]; **ginzo** [or *guinzo*. Also *gingo* (1920). Probably from *guinea*]; **grape-stomper** [used for other Southern Europeans, but especially for Italians]; **greaseball** [1935. Also used for Greeks and other groups]; **greaser** [used especially for Italians]; **guin** [or *ghin, gin,* etc. Shortened from *guinea*]; **guinea** [fixed to Italians by mid-1880s. Or, by 1897, *ginney, ginnee, ginee, guinie,* etc. Cf. *guin*]; **hike** [apparently modeled on *mike*, Irishman]; **italiano; italyite; kike** [mid-1890s. Cf. same word for Jews. Mencken (1963) says used in Pennsylvania mining region]; **lukschen** [also *loksh*. From Yiddish for "noodle," i.e., "spaghetti"]; **macaroni** [also slang for "dude," "fop." A symbol of Italianate things since 18th century]; **mafia** [or *maffia*. 1880s or 1890s. Also rarely, in same period, *black-hand*, from Spanish *mano negra*, and *camorra* (the Neapolitan version of the Mafia) from identical name of blouse worn by members]; **meatball; mediterranean-irish; nickel-nose; organ-grinder** [in British slang since 19th century, but later in U.S.]; **pinocchio** [from Carlo Lorenzini's fairy tale]; **pizon** [probably from slang *paisano*, pal, comrade];

poppie-squalie [possibly from sound of the given name, *Pasqualie*]; **ring-tail** [used also for Japanese]; **shike** [Southern Europeans, especially Italians. Origin not known to me. Cf. *hike*]; **siciliano** [*Sicilian* was a newspaper code for all Italians in the 1920s]; **spag** [shortened from *spaghetti*]; **spaghetti; spaghetti-bender** [also *spaghetti-eater, spaghetti-head*, etc.]; **spic** [or *spik, spick*. Probably from *spig*]; **spig** [until 1915. Probably from *spaghetti*]; **spiggoty** [probably from *spig* or directly from sound of *spaghetti*]; **tally** [probably an alteration of *Italian*]; **tony** [cf. Antonio]; **walliyo** [or *wallio*. Pederson (1964) says probably from Tuscan *guaglione*, boy]; **wino** [Pederson (1964) says used in Chicago and perhaps alludes to use of table wine. Weseen says that identical term is slang for grape pickers and winery workers in the Far West]; **wop** [mid-1890s. Probably clipped form of Neapolitan and Sicilian *guappo*, "dude." See chapter 6].

JAPANESE: **backstabber** [also *stabber-in-the-back*. WWII]; **brownie** [1900. Used in Pacific Northwest]; **cherry-blossom** [fem.]; **dirty-jap** [WWII]; **erb** [a pejorative, like *John*, applied to outgroup persons]; **jap** [c.1865 but more popular after 1902]; **jerkanese** [a blend of *jerk* and *Japanese*]; **jocko** [perhaps from an identical English slang term for a chimpanzee. Cf. *monkeynip*. *Jock* and a jocular form *Jocko* are nicknames for *John*, also a term for any person. Cf. *john* for Chinese, etc.]; **monkeynip** [cf. *nip*]; **nip** [WWII, but older. From *Nippon*]; **ring-tail** [WWII. A derisive term also applied to other groups, especially Italians]; **skibby** [1910. By WWII, the variant *skippy* appeared. Probably from Japanese *sukebei*, lewdness, lechery, and a term used to indicate a lecher. It might have been heard as a salutation of prostitutes]; **slant-eye** [1930s. Also used for other Asian groups]; **tojo** [WWII. From the name of Hideki Tojo, 1885-1948, Japanese general and, in the U.S., a popular symbol of militarism]; **yap** [perhaps only an alteration of *jap*. Yet, Weseen says that an identical *yap*, short for *yaphead* was slang for any stupid, worthless person]; **yellow-bastards** [also *little-yellow-men*, etc. WWII].

NOTE: Most terms for the Japanese originated or became widely known during the Second World War. *Skibby* was the only term widely used in California before the war.

JEWS: **abie** [also *abe*. From Abraham]; **arab** [especially a peddler]; **bagel** [also *jew-bagel*]; **beardie** [19th century. Originally a Jewish convert to Christianity]; **black-peddler** [Northeast Texas use]; **box-of-glue** [rhyming

slang for "Jew"]; **bronx-indian; buttinski** [1902. Probably from a reputation for verbal assertiveness]; **chosen-people** [sometimes burlesqued to
chosen-pipples, chusen-pipples, etc. Cf. *joosh-pipples*]; **christ-killer** [19th
century]; **clipped-dick** [shortened to *clip-dick* and *clip*. Also *cut-cock* and
skinless]; **cloak-and-suiter** [also *suit-and-cloaker, ready-to-wear-set*]; **dave**
[from *David*]; **dirty-jew; eagle-beak** [1939]; **fifteen-two** [also *fifteen-and-
two*. From rhyming slang for "Jew" or from a bettor's phrase]; **ghetto-folk;
go-ghetto** [Roback says from phrase "go-getter"]; **goldberg** [used by
blacks, especially for persons who employ black domestics]; **goose**
[Mencken (1945) says from name of tailor's smoothing iron]; **gypsy** [cf.
arab. Again, probably from old stereotype of wandering and peddling];
hebe [or *heeb*. Mid-1920s. Also *heebie*. All from *Hebrew*]; **hebrew; heeb-
ess** [fem. Burlesque of *Hebrewess*, another slur]; **herring-punisher; hook-
nose** [also *banana-nose,* etc., Cf. *eagle-beak, snozzola*]; **house-of-david-
boy; ikey** [1900. Also *ike*. From *Isaac*]; **ikey-mo** [blend of *ikey* and *Moses*];
israelite [1940s. Especially, black use. Also *israeli, son-of-israel*]; **izzy**
[from *Isadore*]; **jake** [from *Jacob*]; **jap** [fem. Acronym for Jewish-American
Princess. Also masculinized to Prince]; **jew-bastard** [1860s]; **jew-boy**
[1861. Also *yid-kid*]; **jew-norker; jewy, -ie, -ey; joosh-pipples** [cf. the
burlesques of *chosen-people*]; **kike** [1880s. Etymology is greatly disputed.
But probably from Yiddish, *kikel,* circle. See chapter 6]; **kosher-cutie**
[fem.]; **levi; litvak** [especially a Lithuanian Jew]; **max; mocky, -ie** [prob-
ably from Yiddish *makeh,* sore, pest, plague]; **moses; motza** [from the
Passover bread. Early 20th century in London. Later in U.S.]; **motzer**
[rarely, *motzey*. Possibly a variant of *motza*]; **mouchey** [19th century.
Perhaps an alteration of *Moishe*, Moses]; **porker** [also *porky*. Later, variantly, *pork-chopper*]; **rabbi; rachel** [fem.]; **rebecca** [fem.]; **refujew** [espe-
cially refugees from Nazism in 1930s and 1940s]; **sammy** [from Samuel.
Wentworth and Flexner say reinforced by acronym for the Jewish college
fraternity, Sigma Alpha Mu, whose members are called "sammys"];
schon; [19th century. Shortened from Yiddish *schonicker,* peddler];
schonocker [or *schonacker* and other spellings. Alteration of Yiddish
schonicker, peddler. Cf. *shonk* and *shonkey*]; **sheeny, -ey, -ie** [1824. Most
common 1910-25. Origin uncertain. But Wentworth and Flexner say
perhaps from German, *shin,* a petty thief, cheat, miser. Rosten says
perhaps from German-Jewish pronunciation of German *schön,* beautiful,

fine, nice, and a word Jewish peddlers supposedly used to describe the merchandise they offered]; **shonk** [also *shonkey*. Partridge (1970) says shortened from Yiddish *schonicker*, peddler]; **shylock** [also, by folk etymology, *shyster*]; **smous** [also *smouse, smouch, smoutch, schmouser*. Probably from Yiddish *shmues*, talk, chat]; **snozzola** [also *snozzle*. From Yiddish *shnoitsl*, snout, and, in turn, from German *Schnauze*, snout]; **sol** [from Solomon]; **yid** [1915. Offensive when pronounced to rhyme with "did." Sometimes sharpened to *yit*. Also *zhid*, from Russian for "yid"]; **yiddie** [also *yiddle* (1941), *yidden* (1891), *yiddisher*, etc.]; **zaftig** [or *zoftig*. Fem. 1940. From German and Yiddish adjectives, plump, well-rounded, buxom].

KOREANS: **gook; moose** [fem. Originally a prostitute but used for any girl or woman. Flexner (1976) says from Japanese *musume*, girl]; **slant-eye** [especially, fem. Also shortened to *slant* and applied to men, as well]; **slope** [short for *slope-head*].

NOTE: All terms for Koreans are war-related and all were brought forward from World War II and earlier conflicts in the Pacific.

LITHUANIANS: **bohawk** [also *bohak*. Perhaps both are variants of *bohunk*, which, by 1903, was used for most East and Central European groups]; **hunk** [1896. Also *hunky, -ie* (1900)]; **lit** [also *lith*]; **litvak** [or *litvac*. The same term was used among Ashkenazic Jews to designate, with slight pejoration, a Lithuanian Jew]; **lugen** [Pederson (1964) says commonly used in Chicago, but he could not determine the etymology. I suspect it is related to three, probably cognate, slang terms for a newcomer, especially a naive one—*loogan, loogin,* and *luken*, whose origins are not known to me].

MEXICANS: **bean-eater** [1919. Also *bean, beaner, beano*]; **bracero** [c. 1942. From Spanish *bracero*, day laborer]; **brown; cachupin** [19th century]; **chico** [from Spanish *chico*, boy]; **chili-eater** [1919. Also *chili, chili-bean, -belly, -chomper*]; **chili-picker** [1919]; **choctaw** [probably from name of American Indian group, by way of another meaning since 1870s of something unintelligible, as speech or gibberish. Cf. origin of *gringo* for non-Spanish speakers]; **dago** [1832 to 1880s, after which the term attached to Italians]; **dyno** [or *dino*. Cf. *dino* for Italians]; **enchilada-eater; ese** [from border Spanish *ese bato*, that guy]; **frijole-guzzler; frito** [from Spanish *frito*, dish of fried food, perhaps reinforced by the "Frito Bandito" corn-chip commercials]; **gaucho** [from Spanish *gaucho*, cowboy of the Pampas]; **grease-gut** [also *grease-boy*]; **greaser** [1836. Also *greaseball*]; **halfbreed; hombre** [from Spanish *hombre*, man]; **hot-tamale** [fem. 1929]; **mexican-dish** [fem. 1930s]; **mexicano** [or *mejicano*. Also altered to *mescan*. Also *mexican*, shortened to *mex* (1927), *mexie*]; **mick** [an extension of the nickname for the Irish. Catholics in general were called *micks*]; **native** [used in New Mexico]; **never-sweat** [an allusion to laziness]; **oiler** [1907]; **paisano** [from Spanish *paisano*, peasant]; **pelado** [from Spanish *pelado*, a poor ill-bred person]; **peon** [from Spanish *peon*, unskilled farmworker. Especially offensive when pronounced "pee-on"]; **pepper** [1920]; **pepper-belly** [also *pepper-gut*, *hot-pepper-belly*]; **primo** [from Spanish *primo*, dupe]; **sexy-mex** [fem.]; **shuck; spaniard; speedy-gonzales** [from the name of the hero of the ethnic "jokes"]; **spick** [or *spic, spik, spike*. 1915. Same term used for other Latin American and Southern European groups. Traditionally from accented pronunciation of *speak*, as in phrase "No spick Engleesh." But Flexner (1976) says perhaps from cognates *spag* and *spig*, shortened from *spaghetti*, since until 1915, *spig* referred to an Italian]; **sun-grinner; taco-eater** [also *taco-head, taco-bender*]; **tamale; wetback** [1942. Originally an illegal immigrant. From allusion to wet appearance after wading the Rio Grande]; **yellow-belly.**

MORMONS: **mormonites** [19th century].

NORWEGIANS: **herring-destroyer** [also *herring-choker*]; **norsky; scandie; scandiwegian; scoop; scoovy; ski-jumper; skywegian; snooser** [perhaps from *snoose*, from Modern Scandinavian *snus*, shortening of *snustobak(k)*, snuff. Or, more likely, it is a variant of *snoozer* or *snooser*, a 19th-century term for a rascal and a disparaging term for any man]; **sowegian** [1905. Probably from altered blend of Swede and Norwegian. Variantly *scowegian* or *scowwe(e)gian, scowoogian*]; **squarehead; viking.**

NOTE: Several nicknames for Norwegians are also used for Swedes.

PACIFIC ISLANDERS: **brown-brother; brownie, -y; burr-head** [also *burry-head*]; **gee-chee** [or *geechie, gheechee*. Often fem. Also a name for a Eurasian. Wentworth and Flexner say from either Japanese, *geisha*, a female entertainer, or *geechee*, a Bahamian black]; **gook** [Flexner (1976) says possibly from *goo-goo*, a Filipino. Perhaps reinforced by identical word for filth or slime. In the 19th-century U.S., a *gook* was a low-class female prostitute]; **gooney** [1930s. Flexner (1976) says perhaps from a much older dialect word for an albatross. In the 1830s, *goney* was a U.S. term for a simpleton]; **gooney-gal** [fem.]; **grass-skirt** [fem. A Hawaiian]; **hula-lula** [fem. A Hawaiian]; **kanacka** [originally a native of Hawaii. Used on U.S. west coast in 19th century]; **mary** [fem. Pidgin for "woman"]; **monkey-chaser; pineapple** [fem.]; **spick** [or *spic*. See same term for Mexicans. Cf. *spiggotty*]; **spiggotty** [also shortened to *spig*, which may be origin of *spick*]; **squack** [fem. Origin not known to me. Clearly a sound derogation].

NOTE: Most nicknames for Pacific Islanders have war origins. They are rarely applied to these peoples living in the continental United States. They are included nonetheless to complete the list of outgroup nicknames in American English.

PAKISTANIS: **paki.**

POLES: **bohunk** [by 1903, *bohunk* was applied generally to East and Central Europeans, prominently including Polish immigrants. See same under Czechs and Hungarians]; **dumb-polack** [also *dumb-pole*. Cf. *polack* and *pole*]; **dyno** [used in Chicago, especially for a recent immigrant. Pederson (1964) says it is perhaps from sound of Polish *daj-no*, "give"—imperative, second person singular. But cf. *dyno* for Mexicans and *dino* for Italians]; **hunk** [1896. Also *hunky, -ie* (1900). Another general term applied especially to Poles. Cf. *bohunk*. See *hunk* under Hungarians]; **polack** [or *polak, polock* (1879). From Polish *Polak*, an obsolete word for "Pole"]; **polacker** [or *polocker* (1883)]; **pole** [Weingarten lists *pole*, c. 1860, as a slang term for a "Polish person." It is sometimes a metaphor for a dumb person, connoting *dumb-pole*. See Taylor (1974). Cf. *dumb-swede* and similar connotations of *swede*. Perhaps especially offensive when used in the singular]; **poski** [alteration of *Polski*, Pole]; **psecrev** [Pederson (1964) reports it to mean "dogblood." Probably same as Russian slur *psja-krev*, "dog's blood": a Pole]; **stashu** [from the identical Polish given name, i.e., Stanley]; **yak** [Pederson (1964) says it is perhaps from sound of the Polish phrase *Jak sie masz*, "How are you?" More likely, I speculate, it is from slang *yak* or *yack*, a stupid or naive person].

PORTUGUESE: **dago** [used c. 1832 to c. 1887. Thereafter applied principally to Italians. An alteration of Spanish *Diego*, James]; **don** [probably from title *Don* that sometimes precedes given names]; **gese** [or *geese*.

Shortened and altered form of *Portuguese*. Also puns *portugoose, porch-geese*, etc., from sound of *Portuguese*]; **pork-and-beans** [Weekley (1932) and Partridge (1970) say it is a pun on *Portuguese*]; **portergee** [1850. Also *portagee* (1861), *portugee* (1911)].

NOTE: The Portuguese and Spanish were rarely called *spick* and its cognates but these groups were never the chief target of the terms.

PROTESTANTS, WHITE (generic terms): **anglo** [1941. Used by Mexicans and, increasingly, others for Americans of, especially, Anglo-Saxon descent, hence tends to be specific to Protestants. Flexner (1976) says it is "derogatory"]; **left-foot** [also *left-hander*. See Schulman for the universal derogatory connotations of "left." Weseen lists *left-minded* for peculiar, odd, or queer and *left-handed thinker* for one with peculiar ideas. Cf. *right-foot* and *right-hander* as generic terms for Catholics]; **wasp** [1950s. An acronym for *w*hite *A*nglo-*S*axon *P*rotestant].

NOTE: Most nicknames for Protestant religious entities are directed at specific denominations, especially Baptists and Quakers. (*Quaker* itself is a popular nickname for the Religious Society of Friends.) In addition, other more inclusive nicknames are directed at Pentecostal groups, evangelicals, and Southern fundamentalists. See the next entry. Denominationalism also occurs in other religions, though I have never seen it denominated by nicknames.

PROTESTANTS, WHITE (specific terms): **bible-back** [a fundamentalist]; **blue-skin** [Presbyterian. 19th century. From the sense of "blue-laws"]; **broad-brim** [Quaker]; **cohee** [Quaker. Bartlett and others say from mimicking of phrase "Quoth he"]; **dunkard** [Dunker. Also *tunker* (1756). From German, *Tunker*, dipper, i.e., the German Baptists who totally immersed]; **feet-washing-baptist** [certain groups of Fundamentalist Baptists. 1856.]; **forty-gallon-baptist** [certain groups of Fundamentalist Baptists. 1871. An allusion to total immersion]; **free-willer** [a member of the Freewill Baptist Church. 1817]; **hard-shell-baptist** [a member of a conservative wing among Fundamentalist Baptists in the South. The liberal wing was called *soft-shell*]; **holy-roller** [a member of various pentecostal sects noted for ecstatic religiosity]; **jesus-screamer** [also *jesus-shouter*]; **obadiah** [Quaker. 1839. From a common given name]; **quakeress** [fem.]; **shad-belly** [Quaker. 19th century. From the name of an old-style coat, a popular article of dress among Quaker men]; **shaking-quaker** [Shaker. 19th century]; **yellowback** [1878. Specifically a Northern Ireland Protestant. A slang variant of *Orangeman*].

PUERTO RICANS: **chico** [from Spanish *chico*, boy. Formerly a popular personal nickname among Puerto Ricans and Mexicans]; **greaseball** [also *greaser*. Both are general terms used for other Latin American and, in some cases, Southern European groups]; **hatchet-thrower** [black slang]; **hick; nuyorican** [or *newyorican, neorican*. Blends of *New York* and *Puerto Rican*]; **parakeet** [black slang]; **pedro; p.r.** [1950s. Initialism for Puerto Rican]; **rican** [short for Puerto *Rican*]; **speck** [I speculate from *speck, specked*, slang adjectives for something flawed or inferior. Pederson (1964) reported use in Chicago. Cf. *spick*]; **spick** [or *spic*. See entry under Mexicans]; **spill** [a racially mixed Puerto Rican]; **spookerican** [a racially mixed Puerto Rican. A blend of *spook* and Puerto *Rican*].

RUSSIANS: **bear** [from the national symbol and metaphor for Russia]; **bohunk** [used for most Central and East European groups]; **cabbage-eater; candle-eater** [origin not known to me]; **ivan** [also *ivan-ivanovitch*]; **rooshkin** [also *russ*]; **russki, -y** [or *rusky*. 1918]; **slob** [perhaps influenced by spelling and sound of *Slav*. Also *slobovian*. From Al Capp's "Lower Slobovia," a snow-bound land of fur-clad people who spoke with a burlesque Slavic accent]; **steppe-sister** [fem. A pun on *stepsister* and the Russian *Steppes*].

SCOTS: **blue-bonnet** [also *blue-cap*. From an early national costume, a broad, flat bonnet of blue wool]; **jock** [Scottish English for an innocent lad, a country boy, and a nickname for *John*. Also *jockie*, a further diminutive of *jock*]; **kiltie** [1840s. From the wearing of kilts]; **mack** [or *mac*. Probably from prefixes *Mc-* and *Mac-* in many Scottish surnames. Cf. *mac* for the Irish]; **mactavish; pinch-penny** [also *skin-flint, tight-wad*]; **sammy** [origin not known to me. Perhaps from British English term, *sammy*, a fool]; **sandy** [an abbreviation and diminutive of *Alexander*, a popular given name. Also *sawney*, a variant of *sandy*]; **scotchy** [1860. Diminutive of *Scotch*]; **scotty** [19th century. Diminutive of *Scot*]; **saunders** [1832].

SERBS AND CROATS: **itch** [probably from the *-ich* ending of many surnames. Variantly *itchy*. Perhaps influenced by both *itch* and *itchy* in the sense of vermin-infested or lousy. Also *itchycoo*, yet another extension of *itch* and *itchy*, which Franklyn says was influenced by an old ragtime song]; **tug** [origin not known to me. Perhaps from the identical slang term for an uncouth person or from meaning of *tug* as labor, hard work, or toil].

SLOVENES: **krainer** [early 20th century. Variantly *krajner, greiner, griner, grinder*. From *Kranjsko* or, in German, *Krain*, a district in Slovenia from which many early immigrants came. German *Krainer* is a person from that district. See Kess].

SOUTHERNERS (terms used outside the South by whites): **arky, -ie** [originally a poor migrant from Arkansas]; **bible-belter** [1920s. From *bible-belt*, a disparaging term for the South coined by H.L. Mencken]; **butternut** [1860s. From the color of the dye used in home-spun clothing]; **chivalry** [also shortened to *chiv*. Mid 19th century]; **clayeater** [originally poor whites of the lowlands who practiced geophagy. See Bradley]; **cracker** [1784. Originally early settlers of the Piedmont, especially Georgia. Etymology is uncertain. Perhaps from eating cracked corn (and from *corncracker*), from reputation for boastfulness, or from practice of cracking whips. See Presley]; **dixielander; goober-grabber** [19th century. Originally a resident of the peanut-growing states. Probably from Congo *nguba*, a type of peanut]; **good-old-boy** [or *good-ole-boy*]; **hoosier** [see McDavid (1967) and McDavid and McDavid (1973)]; **jeff-davis** [also *jeff*]; **linthead** [1940. Originally a migrant to the North from small Southern mill towns]; **oakie** [1935. Originally a resident of, or a migrant from, Oklahoma, especially from the Dust Bowl during the Depression]; **pike** [also *piker*. 1869. A poor white Southerner outside the South, perhaps one from Pike County, Missouri. See Mencken (1963:707). Or perhaps one who walked the pikes]; **rebel** [also shortened to *reb*. From *johnny-reb*, the most popular nickname for soldiers of the Confederacy]; **redneck** [1915. Probably an allusion to the sunburned necks of farm laborers]; **sharecropper; southern-belle** [fem. Also *belle*]; **southron** [19th century]; **stump-jumper** [originally a poor white rustic]; **white-trash** [19th century. Originally a Southernism used by blacks and whites for poor whites in the region. Also *mean-white*].

NOTE: Most nicknames for white Southerners that were known and used outside the South were terms applied to Southern migrants to other regions of the country in times of economic hardship. Because most white migrants were from the Dust Bowl, the Southern Appalachians, and the depressed mill towns of the Piedmont, these local origins are reflected in the nicknames. Some of the terms are loans from the many Southernisms that were used, within the South, as class epithets. Hundreds of other Southernisms for poor whites and rustics in the South are omitted. Most older black nicknames for whites were, in effect, outgroup nicknames for white Southerners. It is difficult to date when the terms became used as nicknames generally for Southerners, though most emerged as such in the 20th century.

SPANIARDS: **dago** [used c.1832 to c.1887. Thereafter applied principally to Italians. From a corruption of Spanish *Diego*, James]; **jose; spanisher; spinach** [also *spinacher*. Probably from the sound of *Spanish* and *Spanisher*].

SWEDES: **dumbsocks** [Weseen said identical term was slang for any "unintelligent person." *Sock* is an old slang term for "fellow," as in *old-sock*]; **herring-choker** [also *herring-snapper*, which is also a term for a Catholic. *Herring-punisher* is used for Jews]; **olaf; ole; roundhead** [1896. Cf. *squarehead*]; **scandahoovian** [or *scandihuvian*. 1931]; **scandie; scandiwegian; scoop; scoovy; silver-tip; snooser** [see possible etymologies under NOR-WEGIANS]; **sowegian** [1905. Probably an altered blend of *Swede* and *Norwegian*. Variantly *scowegian* or *scowwe(e)gian, scowoogian*]; **squarehead** [late 19th century]; **swede** [also *big-swede, swedie. Swede* is sometimes offensive when used in the singular, for it is a metaphor for a dumb person, connoting *dumb-swede*. See Taylor (1974). Cf. singular *pole* and connotation of *dumb-pole*]; **swenska** [1920. From *Svenska*. Also *swensker, swensky*]; **viking** [also used for Norwegians].

NOTE: Several nicknames for Swedes are also used for Norwegians.

SWISS: **colin-tampon** [Weekley says from "The drum-beat of the Swiss guard"]; **yodellander; yodel(l)er.**

TRI-RACIAL ISOLATES: (Sixty-eight terms for Tri-Racial Isolates are listed in chapter 5, classified by derivation from surnames, place names, putative national origins, historical events, and other allusions.)

TURKS: **abdul; arab; infidel.**

UKRAINIANS: **galician** [1903. Most Ukrainian immigrants were from Galicia. Also used in derogatory sense for any Central European immigrant].

VIETNAMESE: **charlie** [(V.C. was initialism for Viet Cong or simply the Cong. The military communication code for V is *Victor* and C is for *Charlie*, or simply *charlie*, says Flexner (1976). But *charlie* is also an earlier general term for several Asian groups]; **chink; dink** [perhaps a new application of an old identical term for a worthless, unimportant person. Cf. *dink, dink(e)y* for blacks. *Dinge* was rarely used]; **gook** [rejuvenation of the WWII term for Asian groups. Perhaps from *goo-goo* or *gu-gu*. See nicknames for Filipinos. Perhaps influenced by identical word for slime or filth]; **slant-eye** [also shortened to *slant*. Used for other Asian groups since 1930s]. **slope** [short for *slope-head*]; **wog** [possibly from *golliwog*]; **zip** [Flexner (1976) says it probably comes from the army slang acronym *zip* for zero intelligence *potential*. But *zip* is also an old slang term for zero, hence perhaps for anything of small value.].

    NOTE: All nicknames for Vietnamese originated during the Vietnam War or were brought forward from the Korean War and World War II.

WELSH: **cousin-anne** [fem. Originally a wife of a Welsh miner working in the U.S.]; **cousin-jack** [originally a Welsh miner working in the U.S. Note that *cousin-jack* is usually used for the Cornish]; **taffy** [from the sound of Welsh *Daffydd*, i.e., *David, Davy*, a common given name and a sobriquet for St. David, the patron saint of Wales. Also *taffy-mouth*]; **welsher** [also *welshie*. 19th century]; **waler.**

WHITES (used by blacks)—*Color Allusions:* **anemic; bale-of-straw** [usually fem. Also *straw*]; **blondie** [fem.]; **bright-skin** [1920s or earlier]; **chalk; fade; flake** [possibly short for "snowflake." Cf. *snowball*]; **frosty** [from the popular Christmas song "Frosty the Snowman"]; **ghost; golden-girl** [fem.]; **grey** [or *gray*. Also *grey-boy, -dude, -skin, -cat*]; **grey-broad** [fem.]; **lily-white** [1865. Now used with political overtones]; **marshmallow; milk; pale** [also, and perhaps short for, *pale-face*, a term borrowed from hokum Indian talk]; **pale-sault** [fem. Origin of *sault* is not known to me. Perhaps it is an old spelling of *salt*. If so, *salt* was old slang for female genitals, an instance of sexual intercourse and, hence, "a woman." Cf. *scuttle-sault* for a black woman. Also *white-meat*]; **pink** [1900. Also *parlor-pink*]; **pinkie, -y;** [fem.]; **pink-toes** [fem.]; **plain-folks** [19th century. Farmer said "a tit for tat in connection with the term *colored-people*." Clapin says about the same]; **snowball** [cf. *snowball*, a white term for blacks]; **soda-cracker** [perhaps a pun on *cracker* reinforced by the connoted whiteness of the biscuit]; **spook; vanilla.**

Other Physical Differences: **blue-nose** [unclear to me whether an allusion to complexion in cold weather or to prudery, or to both, each reinforcing the other]; **cotton-top; righteous-moss** [reportedly an allusion to whites' hair characteristic, but the allusion is not clear to me]; **silk** [an allusion to whites' hair characteristic]; **silk-broad** [fem.]; **wig; wrinkle-face.**

Group Character and Personality: **algereen** [19th century. Probably from *algerine* (originally an Algerian pirate), a figure of speech for one who acts like a pirate, a tyrant, a terrorist. Cf. *buccaneer*]; **beast; beater; boss** [used in sense of an overbearing, racist white man, and mocked in the phrase "Yowsah, Boss"]; **buccaneer** [19th century or earlier. Perhaps from *buccaneer*, an early pirate slaver in the West Indies]; **buckra** [1730s. Also *buccara, backra, boccra.* Cassidy (1978) says from African Efik *mbakára*, "white man, he who surrounds or governs." Farmer said that *swanga-buckra* was "a negro epithet for a well-dressed white man]; **captain** [also contracted to *cap'n*]; **citizen** [also *republican*, i.e., a "straight," "square," etc.]; **cracker** [same term that whites use for certain Southerners, except in black use it connotes a racist. See *cracker* under SOUTHERNERS]; **devil** [also *white-devil, blue-eyed-devil.* Usually has political overtones]; **hard-head** [probably an allusion to insensitivity and stupidity]; **hinkty** [or *hincty.* Probably from identical slang adjective meaning pompous and overbearing]; **jig-chaser** [a Southern racist, a policeman, or a white who seeks the company of blacks]; **long-knife** [origin not known to me. Perhaps borrowed from old American Indian term for a white soldier]; **lyncher; massa** [from the old slave rendering of *master.* Clapin said it was later "a negro vocative for any white man"]; **mickey-mouse** [not so much from Walt Disney's Mickey Mouse as from the slang sense of petty rules or foolishness. Also shortened to *mickey*, which also suggests *paddy* and *hunkie*]; **redneck** [from the Southern white class epithet but in black use connotes a racist. Also shortened to *'neck*]; **snake** [also *dog* and other terms for "low life"]; **southerner** [also *ku kluxer*].

Black Southernisms that Derided Poor Whites and Rustics: **buttermilk-swallower; cheap-john** [also *john*]; **clay-eater** [see this term under SOUTHERNERS]; **cordwood-cracker; drifter; dude; gillian** [perhaps fem. *Gillian*, informal for *Juliana*, became used for a "wench." *Gillie,* -*ey*, and *giles* were 19th-century slang for a stupid person]; **gulley-digger;**

hay-eater [cf. *clay-eater*]; **hoe-sager** [the allusion of *sager*, a common term for a poor white or rustic, is not known to me]; **leatherneck** [also general slang for any dirty, uncouth person. Cf. *redneck*]; **mean-white**; **no-count** [probably from a dialectal rendering of phrase "of no account"]; **onery** [i.e., "ornery." From dialectal contraction of *ordinary*]; **peckerwood** [or *peckawood*. 1930s. From a dialectal inversion of *woodpecker*, the bird, and a genereal white Southernism for a rustic white. Also shortened to *peck*, which was elaborated to *red-face-peck*]; **pineywood-rooster; poor-white** [1819. Also *poor-white-trash* (1833), *po' buckra, poor-white folks* (1864), *po-it*, presumably a contraction of *poor-white*]; **rebel** [also *old-reb, old-white-reb*. Also *revel*, probably an alteration. From same term for Southerners]; **rosin-chewer** [cf. *clay-eater, hay-eater*]; **saidy-filler** [origin not known to me]; **snuff-dipper** [since the 19th century, snuff-dipping, especially by women, was thought to be a filthy, loathsome habit]; **squatter; tack** [perhaps either short for *tackey*, a poor white, or for *hard-tack*, the food of hard times. Cf. *clay-eater*]; **thin-people** [probably an allusion to the appearance of malnourishment]; **white-arab** [cf. *drifter, squatter*]; **white-trash** [1855]; **wood-hick** [also *yokel* and other terms for a rustic].

Personal Names Used to Redress Urban Status Differences: **charlene** [fem. A term chosen to be a cognate with *charlie*]; **fred; herbie; miss-ann** [fem. 1940s. Also *miss-annie*]; **mister-charlie, -ey** [1930s or earlier. Also *charlie*. Also rendered more "respectfully" as *mr. charles* or *charles* and then reduced to *chuck*. See Abrahams (1970:32)]; **mister-eddie; mister-jones; sylvester** [Major says same meaning as *mister-charlie*. Perhaps from the name of Mel Blanc's ridiculous cartoon character].

Urban Terms of Status Diminution: **faggit** [probably a form of *faggart* or *fag(g)ot*. Also *queer*. I note that *fag* was a slang term for any disliked person]; **honky, -ey, -ie** [1940s or earlier. Probably from a dialectal pronunciation, phonetically spelled, of *hunky*, the term for a Central or East European. Rarely *bohunk*. See chapter 6]; **monkey; paddy** [also *paddy-boy, patty, patty-boy, white-paddy*. Certainly a generalization of the identical term for the Irish. See *paddy* under *IRISH*. Cf. *honky*]; **pig; punk; razor-back; shit-kicker.**

Other Special Social and Cultural Allusions: **ball-face** [used in Boston, 1810-1820. *Ball-face* or *bald-face* was a name for whiskey in the same period]; **dap** [perhaps backslang from *pad*, from *paddy*]; **dem** [also *dey*. From ironic, self-mocking alterations of *them* and *they*]; **face** [1940s. Used especially for a stranger]; **hack; hoople** [origin not known to me]; **kelt** [possibly from an old spelling of *Celt*. Also *keltch*, which seems cognate with *kelt*]; **long-coat** [a comeback for *short-coat*. See *highpockets* for blacks]; **other-man** [1930s. Also *the-man* (1960s)]; **ofay** [or *oofay*. Popular since 1925. Also burlesqued to *ole-fay* or *old-fay*, shortened to *fay*, elaborated to *ofaginzy* and, in 1920s theatrical hog-Latin, *fagingy-fagada*. Possibly from Yoruba *ófé* originally meaning a magical disappearance. See Cassidy (1975) and chapter 6]; **pearls** [fem.]; **spook** [1940s or earlier. Cf. *spook* for blacks]; **star** [fem.]; **wheat-folks** [perhaps *wheat-* is a pun on *white*]; **white-nigger** [or *white-negro*. Early 20th century or earlier. Once a general epithet used against whites, it later was used for a white with black affectations or for a black with white affectations]; **whitey, -ie** [1960s].

YANKEES: **bean-eater** [1800. Specifically a Bostonian]; **blue-bellied-yankee** [Weseen says "an out and out Yankee"]; **damned-yankee; downeaster** [1819. Especially a native of Maine but any New Englander]; **easterner** [19th century, when it referred to Yankees]; **eel** [1837-40. Thornton says from an allusion to slipperiness. In the early 20th century *eel* was slang for a clever person]; **guesser** [1825. Traditionally, from "one who habitually says 'I guess'"]; **jonathan** [1839. An American or a New Englander]; **northerner** [1840. Thornton says "one who lives north of Mason and Dixon's line" and, for Southerners, especially abolitionist Yankees]; **pumpkin-head** [1781. New Englander. Same term was slang for a stupid person]; **round-head** [1781. New Englander]; **swamp-yankee** [originally a rustic Yankee but later generalized to any old-stock New Englander not of the upper classes. See Schell]; **yankee** [1683. See Berrey and Van Den Bark (1953:899-900). McDavid (in his abridgement of Mencken (1963), says it is probably from *Jan Kees*, *Kees* being a diminutive of *Cornelius*, a common Dutch given name, which was the Dutch equivalent of "Joe Doakes" or "John Doe." It seems equally likely that *Yankee(s)* is from the sound of *Jan Kaas*, "John Cheese." Most authorities accept that it is ultimately from *Jan Kaas*, the *s* being taken as a plural inflection. Historically, *yankee* was clearly a derogatory nickname. Originally a derogatory term for Hollanders, later the Dutch of New York turned it on the English of Connecticut, and eventually it was applied to all New Englanders].

NOTE: It is noteworthy that no new terms for Yankees have been coined in well over a century, which suggests a diminishing image of them as a distinctive ethnic group.

CHAPTER 4 **SOCIAL ORIGINS OF THE VOCABULARY**

At this point we proceed to a quantitative, explanatory analysis of the inventory of outgroup nicknames. I am proposing that the number of words for various groups is a consequence of the population composition of the ethnically diverse society and of its ecological implications. This is a sociological interpretation alternative to the usual view that the accumulation of stereotypes and terms of abuse for particular groups basically reflects ethnocentrism and cultural prejudice against them and varies in number with the social distance of each group from the majority. Instead, objective situations of conflict are viewed as preceding both subjective attitudes of hostility and their expression in verbal aggression.

THE DEPENDENT VARIABLE

The dependent variable is the frequency distribution of the 1,078 nicknames for the 57 ethnic categories listed in chapter 3. The terms and, separately, their variants are counted for each group. The number of accumulated terms for a particular group, a value of the dependent variable, represents the variegation of stereotypical images of that group.

These data do not index the frequency or intensity of name-calling against particular groups and they do not represent the frequency or intensity of the use of particular words. The most familiar words probably have been used most frequently, and impressions of their offensiveness today probably indicate the tenor of their use in the past. It cannot be proven, but it seems probable, that the number of nicknames is an indirect index of the frequency and intensity of name-calling against a group. We know that the number of nicknames is associated with, even if not caused by, social distance, ethnocentrism, and prejudice, which do predict the frequency and intensity of name-calling and ethnic slurring in general (Palmore 1962).

A basic fact of name-calling is that almost all groups have been targets and some members of almost all groups have used nicknames for outgroups, regardless of minority or majority status. I am equally certain that majorities originated, borrowed, and used these terms at a greater rate than other groups in the struggle to suppress minorities. Yet the traditional social-problems approach has left an impression that intergroup conflict and name-calling have been directed mostly downwards from majorities toward minorities. All minorities have likely coined, borrowed, and used nick-names for the majorities they contacted, as well as for other minorities.

It could be argued that the sizes of groups influenced scholarly interest in collecting words for particular groups. For example, the early immigration, large size, and subsequent cultural influence of the Irish in American life might have sharpened scholarly eyes for items that at one time denigrated this group. On the other hand, a small group of particularly exotic ways and appearances, greatly despised and roundly named, might be represented by only a few terms in scholarly records. Such an exogenous factor, if it were important, would exaggerate the correlation between group size and the number of terms. But my sense of these data leads me to believe that this factor is small or nonexistent. A greater danger is that scholars have been too thorough in recording nicknames and have sent into print some highly ephemeral words. This factor is also unimportant. I omitted the most obvious of these and subordinated others to "variants," which the analysis separately takes into account.

Coding the Allusions. Each term is coded to the target group, such as Acadians, as shown in chapter 3, and to a category for the stereotype of the group to which the term alludes, such as a stereotype of national character. Coding nicknames to their allusions is an ambiguous and even speculative procedure. Many terms have multiple allusions and reasonably could be coded to two or more categories, if the allusions are at all clear. An independent coding or reliability check probably would yield a slightly different distribution. But I am certain that my generalizations about the stereotypes would remain substantially the same.

The outgroup traits that are most apt to be stereotyped are differences of appearance and of subculture. Many nicknames, which refer primarily to physical and cultural differences between groups, also make secondary references to sex and age. For example, explicit gender references to women derogate both ethnic and sex roles, each by the other. Many nicknames also employ wordplay, such as puns, double entendres, pig Latin, alterations, clippings, blends, nonsense words, and acronyms. A term basically employing a stereotype of (1) *color* might also allude to any (2) *young* (3) *woman* of the group and, in addition, (4) make a *pun*, perhaps involving sex and color, such as *raven-beauty*. The many words with such secondary allusions are coded to the primary physical or subcultural stereotype, such as color or an ethnic food that symbolizes a group.

Variants. In the word list of chapter 3, most lexical variants and some unrelated names expressing identical allusions were subordinated to a "basic" word. Only the basic words, usually the most common, oldest forms, and "autonomous" variants are counted as basic terms. (Table 4.3 will show the number of basic terms for each of the 42 groups and the total number of all terms, adding the variants to the basic terms.) There is much latitude for discretion in these matters and it might appear that this procedure could affect the count for particular groups so much as to bias the correlation coefficients. I use the basic terms for the main correlational procedure. This form of the dependent variable also serves to clarify the lexical inventory for each group. All terms, including the variants, are used in parallel correlation procedures to show that the form of the dependent variable does not affect the findings.

THE INDEPENDENT VARIABLE

The estimation of sizes of ethnic groups is a difficult matter (Price 1980). The need here is to estimate the number of persons in each ethnic category who are most apt to be seen by outsiders as members of that group. The size of identity groups, perhaps the most difficult to estimate, is not pertinent to this study. Nicknames, for the most part, were aimed at persons who were seen as unlike the name-callers. The most alien-seeming persons are those who speak a foreign language, speak English with an accent, are known to be immigrants, have the stigma of racial minority or, for Christian name-callers, are non-Christian in religion. The effective size of most white ethnic groups, for the purposes of this study, is defined as including foreign-born persons who belong to language communities, further circumscribed by country of birth, such as French-speaking immigrants from France.

The U.S. Census offers historical data on country of birth, mother tongue, and race (U.S. Bureau of the Census 1913:992-97; 1933:349-53; 1973:98-123; 1975:116-18). The Census does not ask a question on religion but usually this can be inferred from the conjuncture of country of birth and mother tongue. Other sources are used for estimates of the number of Jews (Gutman 1966; Lazerwitz 1978). For white Christian groups, the most visibly ethnic persons are those who speak a foreign language or who are foreign-born. Actually, visible white ethnicity, such as retention of a traditional mother tongue, might persist into the second generation and even later for some groups.

On the other hand, some white groups, especially if they arrived speaking English, are more apt to lose the public signs of specific ethnicity after the first generation, except perhaps for the emblem of a surname. I have estimated the number of first-generation persons of each group, defined by mother tongue and country of birth. Relative differences in size of most groups would not change greatly if second-generation persons were added.

The racial and religious minorities present a different problem. Racial minorities and Jews, whether for reasons of racial stigma, religious minority, or ethnic persistence, have assimilated less than other groups. Outsiders are more likely to identify these particular persons as members of ethnic groups, regardless of generations removed from immigration. For these reasons, I use estimates of the number of persons of all generations for racial minorities and Jews. All generations of these groups are treated as equivalent to the first generation of other groups.

I found terms for 57 ethnic categories, but there are no usable historical population data for 15 of these. Census data permit size estimates of only 42 specific ethnic groups, and all 42 are among the 106 groups with entries in the *Harvard Encyclopedia of American Ethnic Groups* (Thernstrom, Orlov, and Handlin 1980). The analysis will first treat all 57 categories for which I found terms. I then analyze those 42 groups whose historical size can be estimated from census data. I found no terms for six of the 42, and they are given a value of zero on the dependent variable. I take account of some of the unestimated groups in a supplementary analysis.

The words entered the language at different times, mostly during the past century, in response to the changing ethnic composition of the population.

The value of the independent variable for each of the 42 groups is the mean population size across four decennial censuses—1880, 1910, 1930, and 1970.

Though the availability of certain types of census data influenced the choice of dates, each date fortunately is also significant for the analysis. The figures for 1880 (using of necessity only data for country of birth) index the population composition at the end of the Old Immigration and at the onset of the New Immigration, at the end of the Reconstruction, and during the period of great economic expansion and growth of the industrial city in the North. Estimates for 1910, 1930, and 1970 are based on the mother tongue of the foreign-born, often bounded by the country of birth. The figures for 1910 are more than a generation after 1880, at the apex of the industrial city in the North and Midwest, when the effects of the great New Immigration from eastern and southern Europe were greatly apparent, and perhaps the time when the American city was ethnically most diverse. The census of 1930, another generation later, was after the restriction of immigration in 1924. The U.S. Foreign Stock population also peaked in 1930; the German and Irish Foreign Stock peaked in 1900, but the Italian not until 1940 (Hutchinson 1956:6). The census of 1970 is the ideal cutoff. A new, less restrictive immigration law passed in 1965 began, by the early 1970s, to influence the relative size of some groups; the country is clearly moving into a new era of first-generation ethnic diversity. (I adjusted upward the 1970 census figure for foreign-born Mexicans with federal estimates of the number of illegal or unregistered aliens.) About 1970 is the cutoff also for the word inventory.

THE FINDINGS OF THE STUDY

The principal task of this section is to show the relation of the historical sizes of groups and the numbers of accumulated terms for them. A brief review of the allusions of these words to putative group traits will set the correlational analysis against a more substantive background. In table 4.1 the 1,078 basic terms are broken down into categories and subcategories. The 57 categories of ethnicity (including 4 multi-ethnic aggregates of religion and race) are listed horizontally. Six categories of stereotypical allusions are listed vertically. (See Ehrlich 1973:23-31 for a more general and complete categorization of ethnic stereotypes.) The 53 specific groups

Table 4.1 Number of Nicknames for American Ethnic Groups by Target Group and by Their Allusions

Groups (N = 57)	Physical	Character	Names	Foods	Group Name	Other	Total
Acadians				1	3	3	7
Afro-Americans	105	14	14	3	16	81	233
American Indians	10	5		1	2	11	29
Appalachians		3		1	2	8	14
Arabs					1	2	3
Australians	1	1			2	4	8
Basques					1		1
Belgians					4		4
Bulgarians		1				1	2
Canadians, British					3	3	6
Catholics (generic)		2		2	2	7	13
Chinese	17	1		2	8	10	38
Cornish			2				2
Czechs				1	4	5	10
Dutch		1	2	4	2	5	14
East Indians						2	2
English		2	1	3	4	10	20
Eskimos					7	1	8
Filipinos	2				4	3	9
French			1	2	1	3	7
French Canadians	1		1	5	2	2	11
Germans	1	10	5	7	2	8	33
Greeks		1			1	3	5
Gypsies		3			1	2	6
Hungarians			1	1	4		6
Icelanders						1	1
Irish		8	17	2	2	26	55
Italians		3	6	11	5	20	45
Japanese	3	3			4	6	16
Jews	3	6	14	3	9	29	64
Koreans	2	1				1	4
Lithuanians					2	3	5
Mexicans	3	6	1	12	2	18	42
Mormons					1		1
Norwegians	1			1	5	5	12
Pacific Islanders	3	2		1	1	9	16
Pakistanis					1		1
Poles		1	1		4	5	11
Portuguese			2		3		5

Table 4.1 (continued)

Groups (N = 57)	Physical	Character	Names	Foods	Group Name	Other	Total
Protestants (generic)		1			1	1	3
Protestants (specific)		3	1		4	8	16
Puerto Ricans		4	2		3	4	13
Russians			1	2	2	4	9
Scots		1	5		2	3	11
Serbs & Croats			1			1	2
Slovenes					1		1
Southerners (U.S.)		6		2	3	10	21
Spaniards			2		2		4
Swedes	3	1	2	1	6	4	17
Swiss						3	3
Tri-Racial Isolates	16		13	2		37	68
Turks		1	1			1	3
Ukrainians					1		1
Vietnamese	2				1	5	8
Welsh			2		2	1	5
Whites (by blacks)	32	28	8	5	3	35	111
Yankees		5	1	1		6	13
Total N	205	124	107	76	146	420	1078
Total Row Percents	19.0	11.5	9.9	7.1	13.5	39.0	100.0

compose about half of all American ethnic groups, and include all of the sizable groups. Table 4.1 also indicates the total number of basic terms for each of the 57 categories.

The six categories of outgroup stereotypes and symbols in table 4.1 may be divided into two broad types. *Physical* traits are allusions to color, to shapes of eyes, heads, noses, and lips, and to hair texture. Physical traits account for 205 words, or 19 percent of all words for all groups. Nonphysical or, broadly, cultural traits are allusions to group or national *Character*, personal *Names* (forenames and surnames), ethnic *Foods*, altered proper *Group Names*, and *Other* cultural symbols.

Many but not most interracial terms refer to physical differences. Cultural allusions are more frequent themes, even in name-calling between blacks and whites. This observation requires a modification of Palmore's (1962:443) generalization that "when the outgroup is a different race, most ethnophaulisms expressed stereotyped physical differences." Nonetheless, 45 percent of the 233 terms for blacks refer to physical differences, mostly color, and physical difference is the most prevalent single theme. This is also generally true of terms for Native Americans and the Chinese.

National or group *Character* classifies 124 terms. These include allusions to putative "mental" traits, such as personality, character, intelligence, morality, civility, and political beliefs, and "behavioral" traits, such as grooming, sexual appetite, and demeanor. Personal *Names* categorizes 107 terms derived from given and family names that popularly symbolize a group, such as *pedro* and *murphy*. Some 76 other terms are collected under *Foods*. These are stereotyped notions about national dishes and beverages and about dietary preferences and habits, such as *herring-punisher*, *taco*, or *pepsi*. Altered *Group Names* categorizes 146 terms that derogate by deliberately misnaming with some alteration of the proper group name, such as *frenchy*. Most of these terms are substitutions, misspellings (and phonetically spelled mispronunciations), quaint forms, and other intentional alterations.

The large residual category of *Other* cultural symbols classifies a variety of 420 miscellaneous terms, 39 percent of the total, including terms that are classifiable into about 20 yet smaller but distinct categories, such as references to folk costumes popularly associated with a group. Five of these subsumed categories are large enough to warrant a brief description. First, about 30 terms are symbols of religious differences. Most are generic references to Catholics and Jews; some are specific references to white Protestants. These terms allude to symbols, such as the Cross, Mariolatry, rosaries, the Pope, circumcision, Friday and Lenten fasting, dietary law, and fundamentalist literalism. Second, about 20 terms are various kinds of phonic mimicry that imitate or ridicule accents or that make mocking allusions to stereotyped foreign-language phrases (e.g., *parleyvoo*). Third, about 30 terms refer to stereotypical occupations held in low esteem, such as menial or migrant labor (e.g., *wetback*), or to stigmatized occupations, such as money-lending, huckstering, and peddling (e.g., *shonkey*). Blacks, Jews, Italians, and Mexicans are most often stereotyped with low status occupations. Fourth, about 50 terms refer to low-status places or residences and express the status symbolism of local-community territory. Older terms of rural origin (e.g., *piney*), deride residence on land of small economic value in an agrarian society, such as swamps or brushwoods. More recent terms derogate residence in low-status urban environments, such as slums, ghettos, and cities in general (e.g., *jew-norker*). Finally, about 20 terms simply assert the low status of the outgroup and make no allusion to specific physical or cultural traits, such as *gook, jit, dink, ringtail, honyock, charlie, gooney, zip,* and *white-trash.*

CONTACT, CONFLICT, AND VARIABILITY OF NAMING

In the sections that follow, I first associate the size of ethnic entities with the number of accumulated nicknames for major racial categories, for major religious categories, and then for 42 specific groups. Selected groups are finally examined on a case-by-case basis to specify the historical events and ecological situations that brought each group into contact and conflict with other groups and to explain, informally, the variation unexplained by size. Many of these situations are chronicled vividly and anecdotally by the terms.

Racial Outgroups. Table 4.2-A shows that the numbers of nicknames for broad racial entities have accumulated in the same rank order as these entities are represented in the total U.S. population. While the association is direct, it is also clear that white groups, in the aggregate, have been nicknamed with a disproportionately small variety of terms while blacks have been named with a disproportionately great variety. Further, 18.2 percent of all nicknames have been used for the three percent of the population comprising *Others:* Asian, Pacific, and indigenous Native American groups. Some, however, are war-related terms aimed at Asian and Pacific groups without noticeable concentrations in the continental United States before about 1970.

The largest numbers of terms for specific groups in table 4.1 are the 233 nicknames whites called blacks and the 111 nicknames blacks called whites. Though neither racial category is a single ethnic group, name-callers saw the other stereotypically as a monolith of culture and association. Blacks were the largest minority in the nation and commensurately have the largest number of nicknames. Yet the disproportionately great number of terms for blacks is clearly a result exaggerated by the historical and cultural particulars

Table 4.2 A. Percent of All Nicknames by Major Racial Categories

Race	Percent Total U. S. Population: 1970	Percent All Nicknames	N Nicknames
White	85.0	60.2	649
Black	12.0	21.6	233
Other	3.0	18.2	196
Totals	100.0	100.0	1078

B. Percent of Nicknames for Whites by Major Religious Categories

Religion	Percent U.S. White Population: 1970s[a]	Percent Nicknames for White Groups	N Nicknames
Protestant	63.0	64.0	600[b]
Catholic	27.0	25.6	240
Jewish	3.0	6.8	64
Other White	7.0	3.6	34
Totals	100.0	100.0	938

[a]Estimates from NORC General Social Surveys, 1972-78
[b]200 for the 18 Protestant ethnic groups plus 400 for mostly Protestant poor whites and rustics, excluding 111 terms used by blacks for whites

of slavery and racism. The terms that blacks and whites called each other are the result of a long and bitter interaction, and the history of one set of terms, *mutatis mutandis*, is the history of the other.

The most infamous terms for blacks date from the slave system in the 1600s (Needler 1967). Other nicknames emerged in the 1700s, though most surviving terms appeared in the 1800s and increased in number and bitterness as a result of the Reconstruction and its economic aftermath, when blacks became an agrarian proletariat sometimes in competition with poor Southern whites. Correspondingly, a few of the oldest black terms for whites derive from West African languages (Cassidy 1975; 1978). Other black terms for whites record the oppression of slavery, and many more reflect the poverty and bitter interaction with whites in the rural South (Flexner 1976:53-59). After 1865, a variety of terms were coined for freed slaves (Mencken 1944). Most of the terms that blacks and whites have called one another originated in the rural South and chronicle that era of race relations.

The urbanization of the black population in this century and blacks' emergence as a ghettoized urban proletariat brought them into contact and conflict with many different white groups. White derisions of new black roles in the city are clearly reflected in nicknames for blacks originating after about 1920. These new conflicts, moreover, stimulated the use and persistence of old nicknames from the agrarian South. Correspondingly, there appeared in the cities new black nicknames for whites that expressed resentments toward the new urban relationships, particularly status subordination. (See black terms for whites listed in chapter 3.)

Protestants, Catholics, Jews. The size principle also holds among the three major religious categories in the white population. Most nicknames in the language for white Protestant subgroups or "ethclasses" (Gordon 1963:51-54) are not, strictly speaking, outgroup terms and, for that reason, are not tabulated in table 4.1.

An extraordinary number, 400 to 500, of such ingroup terms have been used, mostly by white Protestants for other Protestant poor whites and rustics. Most of these terms are recorded in five linguistic atlases for the eastern states (McDavid and Witham 1974), the upper Midwest (Allen 1958), and the Gulf States (Pederson 1980). If the idea of "ethclass" is allowed equal status with that of ethnic group in the structural interpretation of intergroup nicknaming, then the 200 terms for the 18 Protestant groups in table 4.1 increase to 600, when a conservative estimate of 400 terms for poor whites and rustics is added.

Table 4.2-B shows that the number of nicknames for Protestants (600), 17 Catholic groups (240), and Jews (64) are in the same order as their respective population sizes. Moreover, the percentages for each category's population size and number of terms are strikingly similar. Whites have called other whites a total of 938 nicknames, which serves as a base N. Protestants are 63 percent of the white population and have been called 64 percent of the terms; Catholics are 27 percent and have been called 26 percent of the terms.

The Jews accumulated twice as many nicknames as would be expected from their relative size. Situational factors, interacting with the historical momentum of anti-Semitism (as in the case of blacks and the historical momentum of racism) resulted in more terms. Some of these might be attributed to the conflict-producing situations of immigrants concentrating in cities of the industrial North, settling in enclaves, and sometimes entering occupations with a public face, such as retailing. But it cannot be argued that Jews differed so greatly from certain other groups in such particulars. The dating of words suggest that ethnic contacts interacted with traditional anti-Semitism to produce a disproportionate variety of terms during the peak period of Ashkenazic immigration, about 1880 to 1910. Moreover, etymologies indicate that some nicknames did not originate in this country, but were originally from Europe. Perhaps a dozen terms for Jews have origins in the Old World languages of Yiddish, German, and Russian.

THE SIZE PRINCIPLE TESTED FOR 42 GROUPS

While the base N for table 4.2-A was the total U.S. population of 203 million in 1970, we now turn to a consideration using a different population base. The independent variable is defined as the number of persons in the first generation of each group, plus the number in all other generations in the case of Jews and racial minorities. This, it was reasoned, estimates the size of the segment of each group that to name-callers is most visibly the ethnic outgroup and the persons who are most likely to be targets. In 1970 this definition comprised 40,459,000 persons or about 20 percent of the total U.S. population. In table 4.3 the first column is the historical size (mean size for 1880, 1910, 1930, 1970). With this population base, the blacks and the Jews are the largest groups and commensurately have been called the greatest variety of names, but not disproportionately so compared to the size of other ethnic entities.

The coefficient of the correlation between the sizes of groups and the numbers of basic terms, excluding variants, for these groups is extremely high ($r = .97$). With a small number of observations, the Pearson r is highly responsive to extreme values, which can obscure or inflate a correlation. For the same reason that a large value dominates a mean with a small number of cases, a large value dominates a Pearson r. The blacks have high values for both population size and the number of names. Yet the ratio of names to population size is about the same for blacks as for other groups (see table 4.3). Thus, the inclusion of blacks does not distort the relationship between names and size, but it does contribute to the extremely high correlation coefficient. When the observation for blacks is dropped from the

Table 4.3 Larger Ethnic Groups by Estimates of Their Mean Population Size (1880, 1910, 1930, and 1970) and by the Number of Nicknames and Their Variants

Groups (N = 42)	Mean Size (in thousands)	Basic Terms	All Terms
Afro-Americans	12,720	233	335
Albanians	4	0	0
American Indians	410	29	39
Arabs	43	3	3
Armenians	28	0	0
Australians	14	8	10
Belgians	39	4	4
Bulgarians	10	2	2
Canadians, British	627	6	9
Chinese	172	38	52
Czechs	146	10	17
Danes	122	0	0
Dutch	110	14	17
East Indians	10	2	3
English	692	20	28
Finns	71	0	0
French	104	7	18
French Canadians	326	11	23
Germans	1,642	33	43
Greeks	125	5	5
Hungarians	163	6	9
Irish	1,050	55	63
Italians	1,028	45	51
Japanese	200	16	18
Jews	3,058	64	91
Lithuanians	100	5	8
Mexicans	1,014	42	57
Norwegians	256	12	15
Poles	594	11	13
Portuguese	56	5	9
Puerto Ricans	289	13	13
Romanians	31	0	0
Scots	238	11	16
Serbs & Croats	80	2	4
Slovaks	123	0	0
Slovenes	55	1	3
Spaniards	35	4	5

Table 4.3 (continued)

Groups (N = 42)	Mean Size (in thousands)	Basic Terms	All Terms
Swedes	406	17	20
Swiss	93	3	3
Turks	8	3	3
Ukrainians	45	1	1
Welsh	60	5	7

correlation, the coefficient falls to $r = .83$ ($r^2 = .69$, N = 41), explaining 69 percent of the variation.

The strength of the basic relation is further clarified by dropping the other three racial minorities—American Indians, Japanese, and Chinese—all of which have more names than expected from their size, especially the Chinese. The coefficient for the 38 observations is $r = .89$, explaining 78 percent of the variation.

A most stringent test of the size hypothesis is to restrict the population to the 34 white Christian groups, each mainly Catholic, Orthodox, or Protestant. The population estimates for the 34 groups are also uniformly based on the number of first-generation persons in the language community. The correlation among white Christian groups is $r = .86$, explaining 74 percent of the variance in the numbers of terms for these groups.

A final procedure demonstrates that defining the dependent variable as the number of basic terms, excluding variants, is a conservative procedure that does not inflate the correlation. When variants (see table 4.3) are added to basic terms (i.e., "All Terms" in table 4.3) to determine values of the dependent variable, the r coefficients cited above increase slightly or remain the same. The conservative coding procedure of subordinating the variants, though it lowers the correlation, better indicates the number of altogether different word images of groups.

All these coefficients indicate "true" correlations for each instance of population and variable definition. How much variation then is explained by the historical size of language communities? It seems conservative to say that about three-quarters of the variation has been explained.

It bears repeating at this point that I am not suggesting that prejudice, ethnocentrism, and social distance are a result only of group size. Rather, the greater numbers of contacts and conflicts with other groups, for which size is a proxy, are factors that variegate expressions of prejudice. Common sense tells us that prejudice has an independent role in determining the number and type of epithets, especially for racial and religious minorities. Racism and anti-Semitism, in particular, are to an extent endemic cultural factors that exist prior to, and independent of, intergroup contact. Contact and conflict activate culturally latent racism and anti-Semitism, and these ideas become the ready substance of verbal aggression against these minorities. Yet these data suggest to me that intergroup contact and conflict also produce and reproduce prejudice, including that which we call racism and anti-Semitism, as well as releasing in expressive forms that which is already there.

SITUATIONAL FACTORS

About three-quarters of the variation in the number of nicknames is explained by the implications of historical group sizes, 1880 to 1970. This final section informally explains some of the unexplained quarter of the variation attributable to other historical and situational factors, mostly ecological and economic variables. A review of historical patterns of inter-group contact, which have combined with group size and its implications to produce more or fewer nicknames for certain groups, clarifies the picture. This also strengthens the size hypothesis by accounting for several groups that for various reasons could not be included in the formal correlational analysis.

Catholic Groups. The Irish were the largest of the early-arriving nine-teenth-century Catholic immigrant groups, and they were profusely nick-named (55 terms). Not all early nicknames for the Irish were directed at the Catholic Irish and it is impossible to know which ones or how many were aimed at the early-arriving Protestant Irish. The Protestant Irish from Ulster immigrated mainly before 1830. They settled in small towns and rural areas of the South and Appalachians. They also identified as "natives" and emerged as the "Scotch-Irish" to distinguish themselves from the later-arriving Catholics (Fallows 1979:19-22). Many of the surviving nicknames for the Irish are very old, some from the eighteenth century, and it is likely that the oldest nicknames were applied originally to the Protestants. For example, Maitland (1891) said that *bog-trotter*, an Irishman, "was formerly applied to the inhabitants of the 'debateable land' on the borders of England and Scotland." Most of the nicknames for the Irish, nonetheless, were directed at the Catholics who arrived in great numbers after 1830. The Irish Catholics, unlike the Protestants, settled in the large and diverse industrial cities of the Northeast and pertinaciously into enclaves. In the late nineteenth and early twentieth centuries the Irish became a major urban proletariat and experienced intense and sustained contact and economic conflict with other groups.

The other early-arriving Catholic group was the southern Germans. (I did not find a single nickname for Austrians and I assume, because of shared language, culture, and sometimes religion, they were not often distinguished from Germans.) The nicknames for Germans do not distinguish between Protestants and Catholics. About one-third of the German immigration was Catholic. Perhaps most nicknames for Germans were inspired by the hostilities of two world wars and this had an obvious halo effect on derogatory terms for German immigrant groups (Seago 1947). German immigrants have disproportionately few names, perhaps because of their frequent Protestantism, some settlement in rural areas, and ways that were seen as agreeably consistent with American values.

The Italians (45 terms) had an immigration experience similar to that of the Irish Catholics, though arriving much later. The number of the Italian Foreign-Stock population peaked in 1940 (Hutchinson 1956:6-7). Many Italian immigrants were from the peasantry of southern Italy and Sicily and settled here in large, isolating enclaves in big northeastern cities. Italian immigrants and their children became a major urban proletariat, and they came into economic conflict and competition with other groups. Many nicknames originated during the peak period of immigration between 1880 and 1930 and some clearly refer to urban occupations and roles.

The Polish for unclear reasons have collected disproportionately few (11) nicknames, although they are relentlessly derogated by other devices (e.g., Welsch 1967; Dundes 1971). Only one term, *polack*, was commonly used and others may be local to the Midwest (Pederson 1964). Certain community factors would seem to predispose the Polish to many contacts and conflicts. Early immigrants settled mainly in big cities in the Northeast and upper Midwest (Hutchinson 1956:26), and they have remained largely big-city and blue-collar (Abramson 1973:34-35, 41). Yet situations conducive to name-calling were perhaps mitigated because the immigration was generally late, in several waves, and more heterogeneous in social class (Lopata 1976:2-4).

The most nicknamed Spanish-speaking groups are the Mexicans in the Southwest and California and the Puerto Ricans in the Northeast. Mexicans, the larger group, have been nicknamed more variously (42 terms) than the Puerto Ricans (13). At least half a dozen terms for Mexicans derive from stereotypes of low-status labor, especially of migrant labor. Some terms for Puerto Ricans reflect cultural prominence in the city and a few reflect evidence of conflict with blacks in adjacent neighborhoods of big cities, such as New York.

The French Canadians and the smaller group of Acadians are groups whose nicknames emerged in the course of a long interaction beginning with the French immigration to Canada in the 1600s and the southward migration of the Acadians in the 1700s. The French Canadians have accumulated a few more nicknames (11) than the Acadians (7), certainly because of their larger size, more urban pattern of settlement (Abramson, 1973:35), and greater concentration in industrial labor, at least in the U.S. The French-speaking Acadians in the rural areas and small towns of Louisiana were called a few of the same nicknames, such as *frog*. The Anglo-Canadians borrowed old nicknames of British origin used for the Continental French and applied them to the early French settlers in Canada. The Americans, in turn, borrowed these terms and used them for immigrants to the industrial towns and cities of New England.

The smaller Catholic and Orthodox groups have accumulated commensurately few or no recorded nicknames. The Lithuanians, with only five terms, are also among the least regionally concentrated Catholic groups and among those least likely to live in big cities (Abramson 1973:29, 34). I found no terms specifically for Slovaks, an urban group slightly larger than the Lithuanians, though they were probably called *hunky*, *bohunk*, and the like (e.g., Nichols 1945). The Greeks are another small group with few nicknames (5) and, as with the Polish, are of several "waves" of immigration; they are also residentially dispersed within and between cities and regions of the country (Moskos 1980:65-66). Greeks also tended to enter small businesses, such as restaurants, rather than industrial labor. I found no terms for the Armenians, an even smaller Orthodox group.

White Protestant Groups. Most descendants of the early-arriving Protestant groups are now seldom seen by others or by themselves as distinct ethnic entities. However, some emerged as subculturally distinct regional groups, differentiated internally by class and denomination (Greeley 1974:253-70). The largest of these regional groups and perhaps the most distinctive is the white Southerners. Killian (1973), Reed (1973), and Tindall (1976) have made a case that white Southerners are a quasi-ethnic group. Dundes (1971) pointed out that the existence of slurs for a folk (i.e., a group) indicates an awareness of a folk and such an awareness may indicate the existence of a folk (i.e., ethnic) culture. Southerners are the largest white Protestant entity toward which specific nicknames are directed.

Regional isolation or lack of contacts with groups other than the blacks accounts for the small number of nicknames for white Southerners before about 1930. The dislocations of the Great Depression and World War II stimulated rural migrations to the cities and brought Southerners into contact with white groups in other regions, which stimulated most of the 21 terms. ("Appalachians," a closely related group, have been called 14 nicknames.) After the war, the migration of Appalachian and other Southern whites to the industrial cities of the Midwest prompted an array of new terms and a revival of old ones. Many, if not most, of the terms used by blacks for whites (table 4.1) referred originally to white Southerners, who were the principal outgroup contact for blacks. If a substantial fraction of terms, probably most, used for whites by blacks $(111 - x)$ are added to the terms for "Appalachians" and Southerners used by other whites (35), then white Southerners and southern highlanders are more variously nicknamed $[(111 - x) + 35]$ than any other white group. Only terms for blacks exceed the number of terms for Southerners calculated in this way. If Southerners had been included in the correlation procedure, this adjustment would set them in rank order and greatly toward the interval distance suggested by their large but undeterminable population size.

The Yankees are the other large regional group with a quasi-ethnic identity that has been called a variety of names. The New England Yankees, unlike the Southerners, have not accumulated a new nickname probably in over one hundred years. Nicknames for Southerners and southern highlanders, on the other hand, are old and new terms that became used by outsiders in this century as the regional isolation of the South and the Appalachian area ended because of world wars, economic depression, and labor migration.

Groups from the British Isles accumulated 38 terms. These groups are now much less distinct than the Continental Protestant groups, such as the Germans and the Scandinavians, and many of the terms are old. Many were used into this century, for old nicknames were kept alive and their use stimulated by continuing immigrations of people from the British Isles. These immigrants, such as the Cornish, were often urban and working-class and competed in the marketplace with similarly placed Catholic groups. Nonetheless, many of the nicknames were applied to the English, Scots, Welsh, Cornish, and Scotch-Irish who immigrated before the rise of the industrial city and who settled mainly in small towns and rural areas, all the while moving westward. When these groups settled in juxtaposition, for all their similarities viewed in retrospect, there were great rivalries and they called one another a great variety of names. These groups soon assimilated with one another and, later, with Protestant groups from northern Europe. Some of the early British-Isles immigrants, mainly the Scotch-Irish, became some of the white Southerners and highlanders considered above. White Protestants have remained disproportionately in small towns and rural areas (Anderson 1970:4-5). This was responsible for some of the cultural conflict between the rural areas and the cities and, correspondingly, pitched the Protestant Nativists against the Catholic, laboring, immigrant masses of the cities (Higham 1963).

Racial Minorities. Racial minorities have disproportionately more nicknames compared to white groups because of the exogenous factor of racism. Yet the size of racial minorities, compared to white groups, is still the principal determinant of the number of terms for them. All native, indigenous groups today number about one million (Wax 1971:27-41) and have been called 37 names, which reflect the history of racism and oppression of these groups. But the Chinese, a group half the size, have as many names (38 terms), because Native Americans, unlike the Chinese, have never been in great and sustained economic competition with whites. Indigenous groups were early relegated to reservations and to other rural areas, often with the poorest and then uncoveted land.

The Chinese are so variously nicknamed because in the nineteenth century they were the largest Asian immigrant minority in the nation, and they were thought to be the "ultimate alien." The terms, many of which date from the 1870s and 1880s, clearly echo the resentments toward the mass immigration for cheap industrial labor, which forced sharp competition with white, native-born labor. Compounding these conflicts with the native-born, the Chinese often settled in big cities and into large and pertinacious enclaves, which heightened their visibility. The late nineteenth century, moreover, was a period of gross ethnic stereotyping and ideological rationalizing that foreshadowed the closing of immigration. Spoehr (1973) argues that in California in the 1870s the exclusionist movement against the Chinese focused on value and cultural conflict, whereas at the same time racist feelings against blacks focused on notions of innate inferiority. These data seem to support this in that, while the terms for both groups are clearly racist, the nicknames for the Chinese lack the animal metaphors and, generally, the rabidity of nicknames for blacks.

The number of nicknames for the Japanese (16) is small, in contrast, though in 1970 the Japanese population exceeded that of the Chinese. Almost all the terms are clearly inspired by the hostilities of World War II (Seago 1947) rather than by domestic conflict, such as economic competition. *Skibby* was the only commonly heard name before the war. In the continental United States, there were almost 140,000 Japanese in 1930 and in 1970 the Japanese population was nearly 600,000. Many Japanese, concentrated in California, became small truck farmers of marginal land and after the war many entered small businesses. Unlike the Chinese, the Japanese in the continental United States have never been a large, visible urban proletariat seen as a threat to the jobs and wage rates of native-born labor.

The Filipinos, the next smaller racial minority, with a Foreign Stock population of between 200,000 and 300,000 in 1970, have nine nicknames. Similarly, Korean and Southeast Asian groups, commensurate with their even smaller numbers, have accumulated few or no terms stemming from domestic conflicts.

CONCLUDING REMARKS

Ethnocentrism and prejudice toward outgroups, indexed by the variety of nicknames, result in large part from historical intergroup contact, interaction, and conflict in situations of economic competition, often in the local community. The number and variety of nicknames signify more than a symptom of prejudice and an attendant social problem. Normative concerns, an emphasis on minorities as victims, and a singular focus on racial and immigrant ethnicity have fostered an empirically unwarranted impression of the nature of interethnic conflict. Instead of an image of majority groups unilaterally berating minorities, the study of the full vocabulary of ethnic conflict suggests that the plural society has been more of a back-and-forth struggle and one of shifting equilibria between groups, depending greatly on the fortunes of the economy. Verbal aggression is not only directed "downward" from majorities to repress minorities, but it also flows among similarly situated but competing groups, and is also directed "upward" from minorities to reprove majorities and as a form of protest. Moreover, the study corroborates that the struggles among ethnic groups have a great deal to do with class and status.

A basic fact emphasized by this study is that almost all groups in the plural society have been involved in name-making, name-calling—and being called names. Less obvious is that ethnic groups are nicknamed with a variety of terms in direct proportion to their aggregate contacts with other groups and not primarily as an inverse function of diminishing minority status. The largest majority and the largest minority groups have had the greatest number of contact points with other groups, which have spawned a commensurate number of different words for them. Nonetheless, racism, anti-Semitism, anti-Catholicism, and other standing cultural prejudices have aggravated the conflict at these points of contact.

Any distraction from the idea that the roots of prejudice do not all lie within the prejudiced is forever open to the charge of "blaming the victim." I am not suggesting that groups somehow attract the unjust advances of prejudice and hostility simply because they are numerous. Rather, groups have many points of contact because they are numerous, hence under certain conditions enter into *conflict* with other groups over specific issues. Size and contact are not themselves the problem. It is conflict that in large part produces prejudice. And the amelioration of prejudice will largely be in the relief of conflict.

CHAPTER 5 **TERMS FOR MARGINAL PERSONS AND GROUPS**

Familiarity breeds contempt—and children.—Mark Twain, from the *Notebooks*

The mission of the United States is one of benevolent assimilation.—President William McKinley, 1843-1901

Most nicknames for ethnic groups—those in the lists in chapter 3—specify fairly distinct, bounded, traditional, culturally coherent social entities, mostly groups of a single national origin. That vocabulary might be said to classify the stable, patterned aspects of ethnic diversity. Ethnicity is also a dynamic process of change and emergence, and many additional terms presented in this chapter were used to name persons who were ethnically marginal to established groups.

Gordon (1963) and others have studied the process and meaning of assimilation in American society. I use the idea of assimilation here in the broadest scope of all its meanings, ranging from the smallest acculturation all the way to amalgamation through interethnic marriage and to the often marginal status of the descendants of those unions. Assimilation in this broadest sense includes cultural, behavioral, identificational, structural, associational, marital, and genetic mergence of one group into one or more other groups or into wholly new ethnic entities. Historically, most but not all assimilation in North America has been toward the majority and dominant mainstream of middle-class, white, Protestant, Anglo-Saxon ethnicity.

At any given time in American history, the people who are assimilating or who are identifiably of recent assimilation are few compared to the sizes of the groups they are leaving. Correspondingly, there are fewer terms that name persons of these marginal statuses than name persons in established ethnic groups. Just as the examination of names for established groups shows how the dynamic of ethnic contact and conflict has to do with class and status, so the study of nicknames for assimilators shows that class and status are the central issues arising from the conflict of assimilation. Assimilation in America historically has been associated with upward social mobility and this is clearly reflected in names for these persons.

From the viewpoint of name-callers, assimilators are deviants from group norms. Often others in the same group call them names in an effort to censure, to exert social control, to rank order, and to detract from their moral authority. In the case of descendants of racially unlike parents, the targets are often viewed by the dominant group as so alien as to be altogether outgroups. Derision, pejoration, and derogation also are aimed at ethnic apostates who have spurned or not fully met the normative expectations of their group. These words indicate culture clash and conflict within groups.

Abusive terms for persons and groups that are ethnically marginal can be divided into three broad classes. First, there are terms for racially mixed persons and groups. These include terms for descendants of black and white unions and for communities of Tri-Racial Isolates. These words are mostly for outgroups, but some are used within groups. Second, there are terms that scold persons who are socially assimilating, and most of these are ingroup terms. Third, there are terms, mostly ingroup, that simply point to low status within the group.

NICKNAMES FOR RACIALLY MIXED PERSONS AND GROUPS

The most ambiguous and paradoxical state of ethnic marginality is that of racially mixed persons, that is, descendants of parents thought to be racially unlike. Such individuals are often in the untenable position of being regarded as an outgroup person by both groups of origin, regardless of whether they identify with one or the other. The majority usually relegates them to the minority. At best, they are partially accepted by one group, usually the minority. In some cases, they have been set apart and have formed separate communities and identities, notably some 200 communities of Tri-Racial Isolates in the eastern United States.

The condition of racial and ethnic marginality has for centuries seized the literary imagination and, in this century, the sociological imagination. It is emotionally powerful material, and persons and groups in this situation have been classified, labeled, and derogated with an extraordinarily various and vivid vocabulary. In North America, most unions between racially unlike persons have been between blacks and whites, less often between other groups.

There is no perfect term for racially mixed persons. Ideally, one would not be necessary, but social reality assures that words will be used. *Interracial* sounds at once gratuitous, euphemistic, and jargonish. An alternative is the adjective *mixed* in various phrases, such as in "mixed parentage," "ethnically mixed," and so on. *Mixed*, however, has long had pejorative connotations. Yet it is parallel to, and has a precedent in, Spanish *mestizo* (of mixed race), which derives from Old Spanish, and now refers to cultural as well as racial amalgamation. *Mestizo* in modern Spanish usually has no derogatory connotations in distinguishing the majority of Latin Americans from the indigenous peoples, on the on hand, and people of European descent, on the other. Of course, naming racial persons with old Spanish and Portuguese words, such as *negro*, has a bad history (e.g., Moore 1960; Bennett 1969). But, for the purpose at hand, *mixed* seems the most acceptable.

Descendants of Black and White Unions. Most terms for racially mixed persons refer to descendants of black and white unions. Many of the older terms derive from Louisiana French and American Spanish.

The most common term is *mulatto*. Mencken (1944) thought that *mulatto*, along with *quadroon* [from Spanish *cuarterón*, quarter] and *octoroon* [*octo* + *roon*, modeled on *quadroon*], was disappearing from American speech, but that was not to be the case. Curiously, *mulatto* has a measure of acceptability among blacks, whites, and even among the persons it designates. *Mulatto* is now sometimes used in the printed mass media, apparently without pejoration (e.g., Coombs 1978).

It is an old word used in British English since the sixteenth century. By the seventeenth century, *mulatto* appeared in American English to mean a person of black and white ancestry, usually half and half. Compounding racial insult with sexual insult, a woman was called a *mulatress*, a pejorative appearing at the beginning of the nineteenth century. In the past, *mulatto* has been variantly spelled *malatta, melatto, muletto, mulattoe*, and probably other ways (Mencken 1944). It derives from the Spanish and Portuguese *mulo*, in its diminutive form *mulato*, a young mule. *Mulatto* then is an animal metaphor, which is one of the meaner devices in making ethnic slurs. If it were still used with its etymological connotations, *mulatto* would be among the most insulting of terms. It surely originated as a derogatory allusion to mixed parentage and later in addition may have alluded to the negative image of the mule as a low beast of burden.

In the early nineteenth century, white Americans, particularly in the South, seemed nearly obsessed with the physical variegation resulting from the amalgamation of blacks and whites. This preoccupation is reflected in lexical taxonomies that purported to denominate persons of different degrees of racial mixture. John Russell Bartlett and other nineteenth-century lexicographers reported these terms as Americanisms.

One system, reportedly used in New Orleans early in the nineteenth century claimed to specify the exact proportion of black "blood" in racially mixed persons: *mulatto*, one-half black; *quadroon* [or *quarteroon*, *quarteron*, *cuarteroon*, all from Spanish *cuarterón*, quarter, quadroon], one-quarter black; *métis* [1817. From Old French, (of) mixed breed, mongrel, half-breed], one-eighth black; *meamelouc* [origin uncertain. Clapin (1902) says it derives from *mameluke*, a slave in a Muslim country], one-sixteenth black; *demi-meamelouc*, one-thirty-second black; *sang-mêle*, one-sixty-fourth black; *griffe* [from Louisiana French and Spanish *grifo*, curly haired], three-quarters black; *marabou* [origin uncertain, but perhaps from Louisiana French, *marabout*. Cf. *meamelouc*], five-eighths black; *sacaira* [OED says of "obscure origin," but possibly from Old French], seven-eighths black. *Métis*, one of the more widely used terms, variegated to *metice*. The feminine form of *métis*, *métisse*, was used in the 1790s and later.

Yet other taxonomies have ranged from official government designations to the locutions of parlor politesse. Mencken (1963:384-85) reports that, before 1890, the U.S. Bureau of the Census categorized black Americans, in descending order, as: *black*, full African; *mulatto*, half black; *quadroon*, quarter black; *octoroon*, eighth black; and *griffe*, one-sixteenth or less black. In 1891, Booker T. Washington persuaded the Census Bureau to drop this odious taxonomy and to classify black Americans by the single term *Negro*. Mencken (1963:385), on the other hand, reports a graduated taxonomy that was understood among whites in Memphis: (1) *black* (from when it was an epithet); (2) *dark-brown*; (3) *light-brown*; (4) *olive*; (5) *meriny* (rhymes with *tiny*, and Mencken asks: "from the curly wool of the Merino sheep?"); (6) *fair*.

Mestizo, from Spanish meaning of mixed race, variegated to *mestee* and *mustee* early in the eighteenth century. *Mustee*, as *musta*, combined with Spanish *fino*, fine, to become *mustafino*, a fine "mustee." *Griffe*, from *grifo*, variegated to *griff*. Other etymologically related terms, *griffen, griffon, griffane, griffone*, etc., might be varieties of French *griffon*, griffin, the fabled creature with the head of an eagle and the body of a lion, whose name was popularly applied to anything that seemed half and half. The terms eventually lost their supposed fractional precision and came to refer to any mix. Most were obsolete by the end of the nineteenth century. In the twentieth century *mulatto* came to mean a racially mixed person of any "proportion."

A larger variety of terms for descendants of black and white unions were Americanisms more home-grown in American English. Like some of the nicknames called between blacks and whites, it is impossible to determine in which group many of the terms originated, though it is clear that they were often borrowed between black and white usage. It is noteworthy that most of these words use color allusions.

The lexicographical sources indicate that some terms were used particularly for women, especially young attractive women. The following terms were marked by sources as applying especially to women: *banana; bird's-eye-maple; brown-girl; high-yellow* [dialectally rendered to *-yeller* and *-yallar*]; *lemon; mulatto-meat; peola* [origin not known to me]; *pink-toes; pinky, -ie; redbone; yellow-girl* [1860s]; and *yola* [perhaps an alteration of *yellow*].

Other terms are not marked gender specific, though my sense is that most were usually applied to men and less often included women: *beige; black-and-tan* [also *brown-and-tan; bleached-ebony; brass-ankle* [1931]; *brown* [19th century]; *brown-polish* [1900]; *beginner-brown; bright* [1831, also *bright-mulatto*]; *crap-yellow; creole* [1800]; *half-white* [also *half-breed, part-white*]; *headlight* [1920s]; *high-brown* [also *light-brown*]; *kelt* [and *keltch*. 1920s. Also *three-quarters-kelt*, or *-keltch*]; *mahogany; mustard-yellow; punkin-yellow; sepe* [also *sepia* and *sepian*]; *spill* [specifically a Puerto Rican]; *spookerican* [c. 1950. A Puerto Rican]; *tan; white-nigger; yellow* [1814.

Dialectally *yaller* and *yeller*]; *yellow-back*; *zebra*. The number of terms known to have been used by both blacks and whites or used primarily by whites is small in comparison to the elaboration of ingroup color names that were used, with rare exceptions, by blacks; these are discussed in a later section on terms for status within groups.

The Tri-Racial Isolates. Only a few terms refer to bi-ethnic Indian-white and black-Indian mixes. The only terms for Indian and white mixes are *half-breed* [1775], *quarter-breed* [1862], and *cross-breed*, all of which have been shortened to *breed*. *Griffe* was occasionally used for a black and Indian mix. Most racially mixed descendents of these original groups long ago passed into one of these three racial categories. But communities of Tri-Racial Isolates have been denominated with as many as 68 terms, and there are undoubtedly others. These refer to racially mixed groups who live in scattered settlements of persons of various Native American Indian, black, and white ancestry.

For various historical reasons some descendents of these mixed unions, many of them tri-racial mixes, settled into more than 200 small, rural, and isolated communities in the eastern United States. Many of these local settlements soon acquired local names. Some of these names derive from surnames prevalent in the communities and from the names of places where the groups live. Other names for Tri-Racial Isolates reflect the same themes of outgroup derogation as terms for other groups.

Dunlap and Weslager (1947), Berry (1963), and others studied the origins of names for these groups and noted 68 terms and their etymologies. Some of the names apply to several different settlements, which accounts for some of the discrepancy between the number of communities and the number of terms (there are more than 200 communities and only 68 terms). *Melungeon* [or *malungeon*] is probably the best known of these names, and it designates several related communities. A few of the names, or some version of them, have been taken by some groups as their proper name, the groups having no other nominal ethnic identity.

Though these groups, taken together, have no single, widely accepted proper name, scholars have used terms such as *mixed-blood*. Genteel regional writers have referred to them with names such as *mystery-people*, referring to their obscure origins, *raceless-people*, and *racial-orphans*. They also have been referred to as *local-mixed-groups, mixed-blood-racial-islands,* and, unkindly, as *half-castes, half-breeds,* or just *breeds.* Estabrook and McDougle (1926) coined the acronym WIN, apparently for White, Indian, and Negro, as a pseudonym for one such community. Berry (1963) suggests borrowing the Spanish *mestizo.* But the jargonish term *Tri-Racial-Isolates* has favor among most academics who write about these communities.

Most of the local, informal terms leveled at these communities are derogatory. (Certain names, such as *our-people* and others, are applied by the groups to themselves without pejoration.) While nicknames for these people are a product of intergroup contact and conflict, they are an exception to the principle that the coinage of outgroup nicknames flourishes where many different groups are in forced, close contact, such as at the center of an industrial city. Each community, sometimes including a few nearby communities, has been given a separate nickname. The proliferation of nicknaming occurs, not because the outgroup is large and compact, but because its communities are small and geographically so widely dispersed as to be seen as separate communities and thus as separate peoples. The isolation of these communities and their particular origins and histories also produce distinctive subcultures or variegated ethnicity. The explanation for the large variety of terms nonetheless lies with the demographic and ecological situations of the groups rather than just with the prejudice of the name-callers.

The allusions of these terms are similar to those of nicknames for other groups. Allusion to dark color is a frequent but not a dominant theme. Certain other themes are noteworthy.

About a dozen nicknames derive from, sometimes as alterations of, patronymic names of clans thought to predominate in these communities: *bones* [probably from *Boone,* but possibly short for *red-bones*]; *chavises; clappers; coe-clan; collinses; creels* [possibly a variant of *creoles*]; *goins; goulds* [also *gould-towners*]; *laster-tribe; males* [possibly from *Mayle, Mail, or Mahle*]; *pools* [from *Vanderpool*]; *slowters* [from *Slaughter*]; and *vanguilders* (see Berry 1963).

A score of nicknames for other groups derive from place names: *adamstown-indians; black-waterites* [or *black-waters*]; *cane-river-mulattoes; carmel-indians; cecil-indians* [or *cecilville-indians*]; *croatans* [or *croatan-indians.* Very offensive when shortened to *cros,* i.e., "crows"]; *g.-and-b.-indians* [from the initials of the Grafton and Belington Railroad]; *haliwa-indians; keating-mountain-group; marlboro-blues; pea-ridge-group; person-county-indians; ramapo-people; ridgemanites; sabines; sand-hill-indians; summerville-indians; west-hill-indians.*

Yet other groups are named after actual nationalities, whose names are symbols widely applied to notably foreign, especially dark people: *arabs; cajuns; creoles; cubans; greeks; guineas; moors; portuguese;* and *turks.* In the word list in chapter 3, several of these terms—*arab, greek, guinea,* and *turk*—were associated with groups as various as blacks, Italians, Irish, and Jews.

A few groups have especially derogatory nicknames, which are used generally for mixed persons: *breed; creole; half-caste;* and *half-nigger.* Half a dozen terms make direct allusion to color: *blue-eyed-negroes; brown-people; red-bones* [possibly from a folk belief that Native American Indians have bones with a reddish hue]; *red-legs; red-nigger; yellow-people;* and *yellow-hammers* [*Hammer* is an old term of general derogation, possibly reinforced in this usage by "yellow." Also *yellow-hammer* is a term for the yellow-shafted flicker. Cf. *peckerwood*].

A few nicknames echo historical events, such as *issues,* which is short for "free-issue"—a free-born black before the Civil War. This is probably also the origin of *free-jacks,* a term used in the late nineteenth century for any black (Cohen 1972). *Jackson-whites* may be a rendering by folk etymology from *jacks-and-whites,* where *jacks* is short for *free-jacks.* Other names may derive from putative dietary practices, such as *ramps,* possibly from eating ramps, a pungent cousin to the onion, and *clay-eaters,* from alleged geophagy [the same term was applied to certain poor whites in the middle South]. At least one term is said to derive from a phrase: *wesorts,* traditionally from "We sort of people is different." *Bushwacker* is also a term for any rustic.

Etymologies are less certain for other terms. Folk, folkloric, legendary, and traditional etymologies abound. Gilbert (1946) and Dunlap and Weslager (1947) repeat and cite sources for certain speculative etymologies. But Berry (1963) is cautious and concludes that the origin of several, after all, are unknown: *bonackers; brass-ankles* [also a name for any "mulatto"]; *buck-heads; dominickers; hi-los; honies;* and *pond-shiners.* It seems probable that *melungeon* derives from French *mélanger,* to mix; the first-person plural, present indicative is *mélangeons* (Dunlap and Weslager 1947). Or possibly it is related to Afro-Portuguese, *melungo*, shipmate.

TERMS FOR PERSONS WHO ARE SOCIALLY ASSIMILATING

Traitors, it always seems to be said, lose the respect of both sides. In the nineteenth century, a *beardie* was a Jewish convert to Christianity. A *hat-indian* (1898) was a Native who had "become civilized." Recently, *blackneck* is a contemptuous term used in the Deep South for a rural black whose social and political views are thought to be essentially the same as those of his white (*redneck*) counterpart. *Kelt* or *keltch* are old words that, in one of their meanings, expressed contempt for ethnic blacks passing for white. Major (1970) lists *fade*, *faded-boogie* and *white-negro* [or *-nigger*] as having similar meanings. Pederson (1964) says that *narrow-back* is "a second-generation Irishman who has neither the need, the desire, nor the physical equipment to do the work his father had to do." Maitland (1891) described *souper* as "a contemptuous term applied to those Irish Catholics who during the famine conformed, at least outwardly, to Protestantism for the purpose of obtaining soup and other food provided by the narrow bigotry of the age for starving people of the Protestant faith only."

Especially since the black pride movement of the 1960s and the related white ethnic "revival" trend of a few years later, vivid vocabularies have emerged to scold persons who are thought to be assimilating. Many of the words connote ethnic betrayal. In the locutions of the Civil Rights Movement, a variety of nicknames were spin-offs from *uncle-tom*. *Uncle* and *aunt* were diminutives for elderly black men and women since the 1830s and the term *uncle-tom* came into wide use with a variety of meanings after the publication of Harriet Beecher Stowe's *Uncle Tom's Cabin* in 1852. Uncle Tom's reputation today is not wholly deserved. Stowe's character was pious and passive rather than rebellious, but Uncle Tom's character was also revealed when he was repeatedly beaten for refusing to beat other slaves. Later in the story, he died of a beating for refusing to tell the whereabouts of hiding slaves. *Uncle-tom* did not come to mean a subservient black until about 1943 (Flexner 1976:3-4). Since then, particularly in the 1960s, the nickname in this meaning has been shortened to *tom*, made feminine with *aunt-tom* (*aunt-jane* appeared about the same time), updated to *mister-tom* (for an assimilated middle-class black, and probably influenced by *mister-charlie*), and particularized to *doctor-thomas* (for a well-educated, affluent black professional).

Yet other derogatory nicknames were given to blacks thought to be subservient. A few terms may predate 1960, such as *black-fay, handkerchief-head* [1940s. Originally, a black man who wore a "do-rag" to protect his processed hair]; *mickey-mouse; ofay; pancake; sambo;* and *stepin-fetchit* [after the black actor, Stepin Fetchit, who played a ludicrous lackey in 1930s movies]. A verb, *to jeff,* means to fawn over whites. More recent terms are *aunt-jemima* [fem.], *chalker, frosty, gashead* ["gas" might refer to processed hair], *mantan-black* [from the brand name of the sun-tan lotion *Mantan*], and *tonto* [from the name of the Lone Ranger's Indian sidekick].

It was probably not until the 1960s that the nineteenth-century terms *house-nigger* [also coded to the initialism *h.n.*] and *field-nigger* reemerged with the new meanings of passive black and radical black. After about 1968, when *black* began to displace *Negro* as the preferred proper name, the term *Negro* began to connote passivity. The late 1960s heard *oreo* [also *cookie,* after the Nabisco Company's chocolate layer cookie with a white creme filling: "black on the outside but white on the inside"]. Flexner (1976:49) says that *oreo* proved too cute for the blacks and had use mainly among white liberals. *Fudgesickle* (*sic.* But again, as it were, "black on the outside but...") was of the same order and even less successful. The 1960s heard other, similar inventions, such as the pun *afro-saxon* and the acronym *NASP,* for Negro Anglo-Saxon Protestant. Hare (1965:18) in his book *The Black Anglo-Saxons,* quoted the *Washington Afro-American*'s definition of a "Black Anglo-Saxon" as a "moderate" and "an animal who can shuffle his feet and keep his eyes on the ground when he's talking to white people, and at the same time stand up before colored people and demand immediate racial equality."

The media success of *uncle-tom* and *oreo* inspired a bevy of imitations by other groups who felt they shared the black condition. Native American Indians in the 1960s heard *uncle-tommyhawk* and *apple* ("red on the outside but white on the inside"). I have been told that *banana* has been heard in the Chinatowns of San Francisco and New York. The Chicanos borrowed "uncle" for *tío-taco.* Chicanos use several other derogatory terms for assimilators such as *pachuco, pocho,* and *vendido,* and these words are working their way into American slang. *Neoricans* and *newyoricans* [or *nuyoricans*] are used in New York, and in Puerto Rico for young expatriates returning from the mainland, who now speak "Spanglish" and who are thought culturally tainted with big city ways.

A Jew who is thought to have a gentile way of thinking is sometimes called a *goyisher-kop* [literally, a "gentile-head"]. A Yiddish-American slang and secondary meaning of *shiksa* (other than a young gentile woman) is a Jewish girl or woman whose attitudes and behavior resemble those of a gentile. According to Franklyn (1963), the nickname *gaucho* ridicules an Ashkenazic Jew who falsely claims Spanish or Portuguese descent.

Turning "white" is a metaphor used by several white groups referring to assimilation into Anglo-American mainstream culture. For example, the term *white-jew* (in use at least since 1933) is a derogation of an assimilated Jew—especially one who is thought to be studiedly middle-class. Lately, the terms *waspy* and *waspish* have similar connotations. The metaphor of "white" is also turned on some groups by outsiders, as when Canadian Anglophones scold Francophones to "speak white." The term "white," since the nineteenth century (see Farmer 1889 and Thornton 1912:vol. 3), like "right" (versus "left" or "wrong"), is a metaphor for cultural conformity in a plural community, often "Anglo-conformity" to the majority. In the nineteenth century, a *white-Indian* was a "good Indian." Until 1981, an 1830s prophecy in the Book of Mormon was phrased to say that Native American Indians would become "white and delightsome" if they joined the Mormon Church. In slang since the nineteenth century, *white* has meant fair, honest, reliable; a *white-man* was a native, not an alien; a gentile, not a Jew.

Louis Wirth (1928:246-61) in *The Ghetto* relates the vocabulary used by first-generation eastern Jews to designate degrees of assimilation of second generation Jews who, through an ecological succession, by 1915 predominated in Chicago's Lawndale neighborhood. The first-generation residents of the ghetto, symbolized by Maxwell Street, derisively called Lawndale *Deutschland* and its new residents *deitchuks*, for they were thought to emulate the German Jews and their *goyishe* ways. A few residents of Deutschland were *menschen*; they were successful but not assimilated. But most were *al(l)rightnicks*, who were successful and had rejected and betrayed the values and traditions of the ghetto. Rosten (1968:12-14) says that *alrightnik* [the feminine form is *alrightnikeh*] is "pure Yinglish." The suffix *-nik* is added, as with many new Yiddish-Americanisms, to connote scorn and derision. Rosten describes an *alrightnik* as "one who has done 'all right,' and shows it by boasting, ostentation, [and] crude manners—*nouveau riche*, with trimmings."

One must look harder for nicknames that record the strains of assimilation within white Protestant groups, where tensions associated with class, status, and mobility overshadowed those of denominational change. White Protestants have been known to change Protestant denomination as a symbol of upward social mobility. But I found no nicknames that censured this mild apostasy. The Mormons in the nineteenth century were one group whose home-grown ethnic distinctiveness set them as sharply apart as any of the foreign groups. The term *hickory-Mormon* (1855) was probably a term for Mormon assimilators, whom Thornton (1912) described as "those who are half-hearted." In the South, liberal and conservative Baptists called one another—and sometimes themselves—*soft-shell Baptists* and *hard-shell Baptists*.

The act of intergroup socializing was scorned by other nicknames. Blacks scolded blacks who cultivated friendships with whites as *lippie-chaser* and *pink-chaser* [1900-1910] and their white friends were sometimes called *fay*, *jig-chaser* and *white-spot*. *Dark-gable* [a 1940s pun on *Clark Gable*] was a black man who preferred white women. *Greyhounding* [verb] is a black term referring to interracial dating and other socializing.

Whites scolded other whites who socialized with blacks or who were just sympathetic to black causes as *jig-chaser* and *nigger-lover*. In the 1930s, it was probably the slang of whites that dubbed a work gang with both black and white members a *checkerboard-crew*.

Intergroup sexual relations and intermarriage were long scorned by whites. A white man married to a black woman was called a *rhinelander*, the origin of which is not known to me. In the nineteenth-century South, a black mistress of a white man was called a *placee* [from Louisiana French *placée*, "a kept woman"]. A white married to a Native Indian woman, especially if he followed Indian ways, was by 1866 called a *squaw-man*. In U.S. military slang of the 1930s, a *bamboo-American* was a woman of the South Sea Islands who lived with an American service man, who was known as a "shack master." In early Canadian English, a *country-wife* [1829] was an Indian woman married to a white fur trader and a *bit-of-brown* [1831] was an Indian woman kept by a white man in a "country-alliance" (Avis 1967).

Black urban street slang had several terms for interracial couples: *rainbow*; *mod-squad* [from the title of the TV series featuring an integrated team of young detectives]; *zebra*; and *spic-and-span* [for a couple, one Puerto Rican and the other black, and a pun on the brand name of the washing powder].

Most of the above words are ingroup terms that scold assimilators. A few slang terms may be found that are mainly majority-group terms that scold certain minority persons for not assimilating to the mainstream. *Hyphenated-American* has long been an epithet for an ethnic person, especially from the first generation or two of immigrants, who maintains two identities—that of a national ethnic person and that of an American national. Weseen (1934) reported that a *hyphenate* [*hyphen* for short] was a person of "divided allegiance," especially in wartime. (I presume he was alluding to the ambivalence of some German-Americans before World War I.) *Hyphenism*, reports Weseen, is such "a division of allegiance between two countries, especially in wartime."

DISPARAGEMENT OF LOW STATUS WITHIN GROUPS

Large American ethnic groups, as they culturally variegate, develop vocabularies to denominate class and status within the group. The words can be regarded as outgroup nicknames, for they are, in effect, applied to emergent outgroups, though by others of the same general ethnic background. Generally, the larger the immigrant group and the longer their residence in North America, such as the early immigrants from Africa and from the British Isles and northern Europe, the greater the accumulation of nicknames for low-status persons within the group.

Terms Used Among Blacks. Blacks were among the earliest immigrants and, over the course of American history, were the largest minority group. And so blacks developed a large vocabulary to denominate status within the group, especially the terms for invidious color distinctions.

In the nineteenth and early twentieth centuries, extending down to the 1950s, there was in use in black communities an elaborate vocabulary or taxonomy to denote color distinctions and to imply a hierarchy from dark to light and, respectively, from low to high status. Such gradations by the stigmata of color appeared everywhere that European culture and Western colonialism had a substantial influence on non-European peoples. One of the great tragedies of racism in America is that, in the past, blacks applied the logic of white racism, especially the color criterion, to themselves as a system of status. Like other nicknames for American ethnic groups, color code-names were reflected in the popular culture of the mass media (e.g., Van Patten 1931; Otto and Burns 1972). Survey research has revealed the actual extent of this vocabulary in several communities. For example, Charles H. Parrish (1946) determined a hierarchy of 25 color names, recognized by two-thirds of a sample of black college students in Louisville, Kentucky, which ranked status in the black community. In the early 1950s, Parrish and David W. Maurer (Mencken 1963:385, McDavid's annotation) collected in a sample survey more than 200 terms that made color distinctions among blacks.

Lexicographers otherwise have identified some of the terms that were applied to blacks of dark color by other blacks: *blue*; *boot* [Johnson (1972) says *boot* is an allusion to black shoe leather, though I speculate it is a form of *boots*, a late nineteenth-century nickname for a hotel boot-black or shoeshine man. Spears (1981), on the other hand, says it is short for *bootlips*]; *chocolate-to-the-bone* [1920s]; *cluck* [1940s]; *coal-scuttle-blonde [fem.]*; *dewbaby*; *dewskin*; *eightball*; *eightrock*; *midnight*; *oxford*; *shine* [1900-10. Cf. *boot*]; *spade*. In contrast, to take one example, *tush* was an affluent, light-skinned society black person. It is noteworthy that *blue, boot, shine, spade*, among others, may originally have been white terms for blacks.

A few terms refer to other physiognomic features thought incidental to the group, such as *gator-face*; *shad-mouth* [c. 1935]; and *satchel-mouth*. The latter, sometimes shortened to *satchel* and clipped to *satch* and *satchmo*, is best known as an affectionate personal nickname for the late Louis Armstrong.

While these terms of disparagement often ascribed low status in the community, blacks had another, related vocabulary that denominated black social types and special roles in the black community, usually ones held in low esteem.

Some of the names that young black men, especially, call each other are said to be neutral to approving, such as *blood* [early 1970s, shortened from *blood-brother*; also *brother*, *'bro*, *sister*, late 1960s]; the older *brother-in-black*; *boots*; *cuff* [from *cuffey*]; *ham*; *member*; *ned*; *soul-brother* [and *-sister*. 1967]; and *splib*. Other black terms for blacks are implicitly or overtly derogating, such as *butterhead* for an embarassingly stupid person. Black men of traditional demeanor have been called *mose* [1940s], *sam*, and *sambo*. Black women have been called, with various pejorative nuance, *bat*; *booger-bear* [or just *bear*]; *coal-scuttle-blond*; *mullion* [origin not known to me]; and *sapphire*. Various male social types have been called terms such as *clown* [1940s]; *gowster* [or *gouster*. Perhaps originally a drug addict]; *homeboy* [a rural Southern type]; *international-nigger* [a man who wore expensive, foreign-made clothes]; *park-ape* [a rough, ghetto type]; and *street-arab* [a robed Black Muslin in Harlem in the 1960s]. A few terms, such as *gas-head*, *handkerchief-head* [or just *head*], and *slick* were applied to persons thought to have an untoward concern for hair style; each later became a synonym for *uncle-tom*.

Terms Used Within White Groups. In chapter 4, I cited McDavid and Witham (1974), who list many terms, collected for word geographies and in recent use, that whites called other poorer whites, mostly Protestants. Many other older, obsolete terms were used in earlier periods of our history. Nineteenth-century lexicographers of Americanisms list some of these.

Within recently arrived white groups, status derogation sometimes focuses on recency of immigration from abroad. *Greenhorn*, which has meant an inexperienced person since the eighteenth century, was used generally for immigrants by 1917. *Greenhorn* and its variant *greener* was used among the Irish and the Jews. Many groups had at least one nickname for a recent immigrant.

More assimilated groups tended to look down upon the raw recruits. There were original cultural differences as great as religion between the early-arriving Protestant Irish and the later-arriving Catholic Irish. The Protestants, now the so-called Scotch-Irish, set themselves apart from the Catholics at the start. A few of the early nicknames for the Irish, I am certain, were used by the Protestant Irish for the Catholic Irish. Language and other cultural differences separated the early-arriving German Jews and the later-arriving Ashkenazics from Eastern Europe. The antagonism between the German and eastern Jews is famous and gave rise to *buttinski* and *kike*, both later used by outsiders for all Jews. The German Jews also called the Eastern Jews *pollak* (Mencken 1945:614), but the similar *polacker* (1883) and *polak* (direct from Polish) soon attached to Polish Catholics. And there were antagonisms among regional groups of eastern Jews, who referred to one another by such as *litvak* and *galitzianer*, both terms taking on mild derogation (Rosten 1968:124-25, 214-15).

Over time, especially between generations, the subcultural splits within white ethnic groups became ones of class and status. *Bog-trotting, shanty*, and *lace-curtain* were the adjectives that testified to differences among the Irish, especially of Boston. Immigrant white Protestants also became separated by class and elaborately nicknamed, as I mentioned above. In addition, Southern whites have long made distinctions between "quality" people and *white-trash*. *Cracker, hoosier*, and *redneck* are distinctive southern social types held in low esteem (McDavid 1967; McDavid and McDavid 1973). New Englanders similarly distinguish between *brahmins, yankees* and low-status *swamp-yankees* (Schell 1963). And class epithets were sometimes directed upward. In the nineteenth century, especially in New York, *upper-ten-thousand* [1806, often shortened to *upper-ten*], *silk-stocking-gentry* [1812], *uppercrust, brownstoner, plute* [from *plutocrat*], and the contemptuous *tippybobs* echoed class resentments. These people often lived in a part of the city called *nob-hill* [1833], later punned as *snob-hill*. The *nouveau riche* were then sometimes known as the *codfish-aristocracy* [or *-gentility*, 1850], which Bartlett (1877) defined as "a class of people who, with wealth, are too apt to be deficient in intelligence and good manners, and who, nevertheless, assume airs of importance."

Recent migrants to cities, whether from abroad (cf. *greenhorn*) or from our own countryside, are often labeled contemptuously. Most nicknames for white rural-to-urban migrants in this century have been directed at Southerners in northern cities. The great farm-to-city migration that began in the nineteenth century had a late spasm in the depths of the Great Depression. Migrants from the Dust Bowl to Southern California in the 1930s were called *oakie* and *arkie* [-y] and these terms were soon applied to migrants from other places, as well. The beginning of World War II prompted another migration to northern industrial cities. *Hillbilly*, an old term from about 1900, denominated the migrants from the Appalachian region. Migrants from small southern cotton mill towns were called *lint-heads*. After the war, Appalachian whites, now often displaced from the coal mining industry by automation, continued to migrate to the cities of the Ohio Valley and the Midwest. The old terms, *stumpjumper* and *ridgerunner*, used earlier for other rustics and poor whites, again became popular. There was also a new acronymic coinage, *WASP*, in the Chicago slang meaning of White Appalachian Southern Protestant. *Hillbilly* was the only term that really caught on, and its derogation was soon inverted to an ingroup sobriquet, as well.

CONCLUDING REMARKS

The condition of ethnic marginality and the process of assimilation are elaborately detailed by nicknames. Nicknames for marginal persons and groups amply document the strains of assimilation in American life. These terms also result from contact and conflict, often between segments of the same group. The historical cumulation of these nicknames shows that ethnic conflict extends beyond that between wholly unlike groups. Ethnicity is a phenomenon of emergence and new groups are always in the process of becoming. The stages and appearances of the change are described with a vocabulary of anxiety. All the nicknames reprove classes of marginal people, whether marginal as offspring of intergroup unions, marginal through personal assimilation, or marginal by upward mobility, sometimes between generations.

All ethnic name-calling, at bottom, is status disparagement. In the past, persons within a group were sometimes nicknamed for failing to assimilate or to be upwardly mobile. Terms that disparage low status within a broad ethnic category are the oldest and most abundant. Today, persons are more often nicknamed for assimilating or perhaps for assimilating too quickly. Newer terms chide assimilators and apostates who are perceived to deny and betray their ethnic heritage. Ideological thinking in ethnic America is in a trend shifting from a norm of assimilation or "Anglo-conformity" toward a norm of nonassimilation or "pluralism." These words document past, transitional, and achieved phases of this social change.

CHAPTER 6 ETHNIC IDEOLOGY AND
FOLK ETYMOLOGIES

"When I use a word," Humpty Dumpty said in a rather scornful tone, "it means just what I choose it to mean—neither more nor less."

"The question is," said Alice, "whether you *can* make words mean so many different things."

"The question is," said Humpty Dumpty, "which is to be master—that's all."
—Lewis Carroll, from *Through the Looking Glass*

Several well-known nicknames for ethnic groups, such as *wop*, *guinea*, *canuck*, *kike*, *ofay*, *peckerwood*, *honky*, and *gringo*, have inspired many specious etymologies. Some of these fanciful and fantastic stories go beyond the simple confusions of most folk etymologies and are best understood as parables or allegories. They are symbolic narratives with ritual situations of conflict, heroes, villains, and a moral point concerning ethnic relations. Such stories are sometimes invented, believed, and retold by name-callers to justify the derogation, and yet other stories are sometimes invented, believed, and retold by victims to defend against the derogation of the nickname. In either case, these stories reflect ideologically reconstructed histories of intergroup relations. A few of the true or most probable etymologies, as determined by language scholars, suggest even richer stories of conflictful relations in group histories. This final chapter analyzes folk etymologies for eight nicknames and identifies from scholarly sources, when possible, the true etymology.

Etymologists are familiar with many attempts to fill a vacuum of knowledge about the origin or the original allusion of a word with an imaginative guess, often suggested by a similarity of sound or by freely associating an idea. Nicknames for ethnic groups with obscure origins are particularly susceptible to folk etymologies, because they are emotion-laden symbols and seem to demand an explanation that gives ideological consistency and cognitive harmony. These stories, I am suggesting, are a form of ethnic folklore.

In chapter 1, it was argued that nicknames for ethnic outgroups and the sometimes specious etymologies that accompany their use are usefully viewed as folklore. The stock of terms and the folk etymologies known and used by a particular group are elements of a diffuse oral tradition of ingroup lore concerning stereotypes of outgroups. The folk etymologies represent an extension of the semantic lore of the nicknames themselves into complete narratives that serve a variety of social uses similar to those of other ethnic folklores.

Most nicknames are clear allusions to such things as physical differences, exotic ethnic food, emblematic personal and family names, and other popular symbols. But the origin and referents of some popular nicknames are not widely known and speculations abound. Some of the most infamous words have spawned multiple and competing stories regarding their true origin. In most cases, language scholars are in fair agreement about their most probable origin. But specious and spurious stories persist, and they may persist because they serve a purpose.

FOLK ETYMOLOGIES

Folk etymology, a term used in language studies, is narrowly defined as a modification of a word according to a spurious etymology, usually a false analogy to a more familiar word. More broadly, folk etymology may refer to a popular but spurious narrative about the origin of a word. While I am mostly concerned here with the broader definition of folk etymology, I am less concerned with spuriousness than with the social uses of inventing, believing, and repeating this or that story. Contradictory folk etymologies sometimes are competing images of groups in conflict.

Folk etymologies tend to proliferate for the most familiar and widely used, but opaque, nicknames for large groups. The larger the groups involved in conflict and the more sustained the interaction, usually, the more people who have deliberated on the meaning—and the origins—of the words spawned by that conflict. If the allusion of the nickname is not self-evident, and many indirect or altered loanwords from foreign languages are not, a fertile garden for speculation is laid. Folkloric etymologies are useful not only to the name-callers and their victims but also to people who write about the conflict. Some of the stories have been used, if not invented, by popular writers and commentators on the social problems of ethnic relations. A few academics, who are usually obliged to be more cautious, have been tempted to repeat false etymologies, either for convenience or consistency of ideology. It would be incorrect to ascribe impure motives to everyone who has repeated, believed, or even invented specious etymologies. There are issues of genuine professional disagreement among lexicographers and other language scholars. A sociological interpretation nonetheless might help reorder the relative verity of competing etymologies.

A certain zealotry in social science sometimes urges us to analyze the social uses of folklore and to expose its nonfactual basis without much thought to the social injustices that drive people to defend their dignity with spurious beliefs. Folklore about the origin of offensive nicknames, it might be argued, should be left well enough alone. Let the scholars have their most probable etymologies and let the people have the story that best fits their own needs. I am carried into this less by truth and knowledge for their own sake and more by the observation that true etymologies are sometimes more evocative of rich, historical group experience than the folkloric versions.

Users of folk etymologies are naive about how nicknames are loaned between groups, especially between groups in conflict, and how they are sometimes inverted from their original meanings. For example, the outgroup terms *wop*, *kike*, and *peckerwood* were probably first ingroup terms and were later taken by other groups to derogate the whole group in whose garden the term grew. Name-callers have an egoistical urge to assume as their own invention the names they use for outgroups, and they go on to invent or embellish etymologies that support this assumption. This is not usually a conscious action; they presume that a favored word justifiably used by their group must be of internal origin. On the other side of the fence, minority groups who are targets of a nickname, I suspect, tend to resist etymologies that say the term originated within their group. They may prefer to believe stories that have the nicknames gratuitously and meanly imposed upon them by the majority. They feel rightly that they are victims who deserve sympathy, and that the name-callers deserve censure.

Many nicknames are little more than catcalls, the allusions of which have little more meaning than that. But many other nicknames signify the substance and tone of past interactions between groups, and some terms were products of particular events. Persons who identify positively with the group calling a name may with duplicity favor a story that sterilizes its origin so as to imply "no offense." On the other hand, fair-minded persons who identify negatively with name-callers may favor, along with the victims, a story that makes the term a symbol and a product of past injustices. Fanciful and fantastical etymologies are best understood as parables that purport to be fact. They are a folklore of groups in conflict.

In the pages that follow, I give the most probable etymology for each term, based on my reading of scholarly sources. In some cases, the etymology is not certain and I have retold various competing stories. One or more of the stories may have influenced the origin and survival of the word. I will not label any of them wrong, for it is always possible that they are in fact correct or, more likely, that they indicate a dual influence on the emergence of the term. But note the kinds of stories that swirl around these terms.

WOP

Wop, the derogatory and offensive nickname for an Italian, probably derives "from the Neapolitan dialect's *guappo*, a dandy (literally a handsome man), later used as a Neapolitan greeting and by other Italians to refer to a Neapolitan" (Flexner 1976:217). *Webster's Third* (Gove 1961) says it is Neapolitan and Sicilian dialect for "bold, handsome, a bully, a dandy." Roback (1944:70) reported second-hand (from his barber) that *uap* (sic) was often used in Palazzo, between Bari and Calabria, to mean a fop, a swell, a show off, which seems to be about the same meaning as *guappo* and is probably the same word. Anthony Burgess, the British novelist and polyglot, reports that Neapolitans today call themselves *guapi*—the pretty ones. Perhaps the slang term *dude* is the nearest equivalent in American English.

By the mid-1890s, near the peak of Italian immigration to the United States, *wop* appeared in American slang as a derogatory epithet for Italians. In some manner, the Neapolitan and Sicilian dialect's *guappo* was borrowed and the last syllable dropped. Or perhaps the already clipped form that Roback reported was borrowed directly. Most Italian immigrants to the United States came from southern Italy, many from the Naples region. Conceivably, the term was overheard in the banter of Italian immgirants in America and it was taken as a nickname for them (Irwin 1931:196). This would not be unusual, for there are other instances of ingroup sobriquets and greetings being borrowed and turned against a group as a generic name.

A popular but probably wrong story has it that *wop* derives from the acronym for the phrase With Out Papers (or sometimes Passport). There are several versions. Dundes (1971:192), illustrating folk etymology, relates one, "that in the early 1920s many Italians tried to enter the United States illegally. These would-be immigrants were rounded up by U.S. officials and sent back to Italy with documents labeled W.O.P. which supposedly stood for 'Without Papers' referring to the papers needed for legal immigration." Supposedly, for this reason, *wop* became a denomination for such persons and, eventually for Italians in particular. This story, if it is entirely untrue, has the makings of immigration folklore. As the story is variously embellished, the immigrants are pitted against the indifference of immigration officials and the crass bureaucracy of Ellis Island and labelled *wops*, as though they were nonpersons. History tells us that, in fact, many immigrants were processed roughly and meanly. Yet this particular incident, probably only symbolic of the immigration experience, is an obvious allegory for the perceived attitudes of American society in general toward the immigrants.

The With-Out-Papers story for *wop* is seductive because it is consistent with the fact that later nicknames for other groups did emerge from the bureaucratic insensitivities of the host society. Eisiminger (1978) notes that Dr. Max Rafferty, in his syndicated newspaper column of March 17, 1977, reported that 228 readers had sent him this explanation of *wop*. This folkloristic account is so popular that it is worth mentioning why it is probably untrue. First, all immigrants without documentation would have been nicknamed the same, but Italians were the only immigrant group in the 1890s and later who were called *wops*. Unlike other general terms that came to attach particularly to Italians, such as *dago* and *guinea*, there is no record of *wop* having been widely used for any other group. (Weseen [1934], however, reported that *wop* in railroading slang referred to a section hand, "usually a Mexican.") Second, the nickname emerged in American slang in the mid-1890s, before acronyms came into wide use in government bureaucracies, informally or formally. I suspect that the With-Out-Papers (-Passport) story was invented after acronyms and the search for their hidden meanings became popular in the 1930s and 1940s. Finally, I have never seen documentation of this etymology.

While the With-Out-Papers story of *wop* was probably invented inside the Italian community, another story of its origin, and a less imaginative one, was probably invented and fostered by outsiders. Many nicknames for ethnic groups derive from highly visible occupations of the groups. Sometimes specious etymologies also take inspiration from occupational stereotypes of a group. For example, there have been stories that the origin of *greaser* and *oiler* for Mexicans derived from the occupation of oiling or greasing the wheels of trains in the railway industry. Similarly, there is a popular story among non-Italians that *wop* derives from an acronym for the phrase Work On Pavement, probably inspired by the occupational stereotype of Italians as concentrated in the masonry, construction, and road-building industries.

Useful stories die hard. The With-Out-Papers story of *wop* seems to have served a need for some Italians. The Work-On-Pavement story serves a purpose for some non-Italians, such as trying to render less offensive or obscure a derogatory epithet. Folk etymologies can be used to arbitrate interethnic conflict. There are a few news stories of court judges, in presiding over assault cases and other conflicts with ethnic overtones, who have ruled upon the offensiveness of nicknames allegedly used as provocation to the conflict. In order to rule that the use of a particular epithet is not a justifiable provocation to an assault, the meaning and the etymology of the nickname has to be made less offensive. Reportedly, the Work-On-Pavement story of the origin of *wop* was judicially decreed in Brome-Missisquoi County, Quebec, as verity and thus *wop* was not offensive enough to be provocation to assault.

GUINEA

Guinea, a nickname for Italians that appeared in the 1880s, does not have a certain explanation of why it is now applied only to Italians. The term was in the language before it was applied to Italians and two influences probably account for its early meaning. First, the *Dictionary of American English* gives one meaning, among others, of *guinea* as "any unknown or distant country." Second, Flexner (1976:217) reports that *guinea* was in 1789 a term for a black slave from the Guinea Coast of Africa and that (p. 55) the word later came to mean "any large, strong, or mean slave." *Webster's Third* gives one definition of *guinea* as "a person notably foreign." It is possible that *guinea* was applied to Italians, and early on possibly also to other immigrant groups, as an expression of contempt. By the 1920s, several variants, such as *guin* and *guinzo*, relentlessly attached to Italians.

Such a popular term often demands a more satisfying explanation and at least one has appeared. Roback (1944:37) repeated but did not endorse a story that has the tenor of folk etymology, a condescending tale invented by non-Italians: "According to some, the slur goes back to the time when English pennies were circulating in North America, and during a crisis, Italian help would receive them for services. The pennies were called 'guineas' in jest. Later, the name was transferred to the recipients, who, it is said, collected these pennies as valuable coins."

KIKE

By the mid-1880s, *kike* had emerged as a nickname for Jews. Its origin is uncertain, though half a dozen stories claim to account for it. *The Random House Dictionary of the English Language* (Stein and Urdang 1966) blandly said *kike* was "apparently, modeled on *hike*, an Italian, itself modeled on *mike*, Irishman, short for Michael." It may be as simple as this, but there are several other stories that deserve retelling, one or two of which seem likely. There is general agreement that it derives from American Yiddish slang. And there is agreement that it was originally an ingroup term used by the early-arrived "German" Jews to denominate the Ashkenazic Jews who arrived around the turn of the last century. Otherwise, speculations about the origin of *kike* have abounded since early in this century.

One etymology, first hinted in 1934 by *Webster's Second* and repeated by Mencken (1936), is that *kike* "may have some relation to *keek*, a term used in the clothing trade to designate one employed to spy out the designs of rival manufacturers. *Keek* is an ancient English verb, now confined to Northern dialects, signifying to peep. Its past tense form appears in Chaucer's 'Miller's Tale' (c.1386) as *kiked.*" *Keek* in the sense of a fashion spy was recorded in the *Century Dictionary and Cyclopedia*, Supplement, 1911. Weseen (1934) lists both *keek* and, separately, *kyke* (*sic*) as a manufacturer's spy, especially in the clothing industry; *kike*, a Jew, is a third listing. Rabbi Jacob Tarlau, one of Mencken's (1945:614-15) correspondents, wrote that he could not see how *keek* in the context of the clothing business that was dominated by German Jews and non-Jews long after the influx of Russian Jews, could have spawned *kike*; perhaps *kuck* or *kucker*, but hardly *kike*. Tarlau went on to say that he liked to think that *kike* may have come from the Yiddish *kek*, cake, pronounced in the Galician way of making the long German vowel *e* into *ei*. But that is surely fanciful. Tamony (1977) favors the etymology from *keek* and believes, moreover, that the use of *kike* was reinforced by the sound of the derogatory nicknames *ike* and *ikey* from *Issac* and other coincidences.

Lacher (1926) thought *kike* was suggested by the many Ashkenazic surnames ending in -*(s)ki* and -*(s)ky*. According to Lacher, some German-Jewish traveling men designated their competitors contemptuously as *kikis*, which was contracted to *kikes*. Mencken repeated but never accepted this etymology; Tamony (1977) dismisses it as folk etymology. Yet *Webster's Third* (Gove 1961) largely accepts this version and says that *kike* is probably an alteration of *kiki*, a reduplication of -*ki*, the common ending of names of Jews who lives in Slavic countries. One obvious flaw is that the *s*'s in -*(s)ki* and -*(s)ky* are not accounted for in Lacher's story. As Tamony notes, the full -*ski* pops up in another nickname for Eastern Jews, *buttinski*. (The reduplicative device, *kiki*, is also popularly used with other meanings and may have influenced stories of the origin of *kike*. In addition to being a diminutive nickname for girls and women, *kiki* has recently emerged as a voguish contraction of "*k*ind of this, *k*ind of that," a humorous self-descriptive used by a few lesbian women [Homer 1979].) The Lacher story persists, and writers such as Glanz (1964:70), Birmingham (1967:291ff), and Dohan (1974:249) repeat it without qualification. But it is clear that *kike* emerged as a general status derogation among Jews, regardless of how surnames ended. Abraham Cahan (1917) had one of his characters in *The Rise of David Levinsky* say "You know who Mr. Levinsky is, don't you. It isn't some kike. It's David Levinsky, the cloak manufacturer...."

Another possible etymology is that *kike* derives from Yiddish *kikel*, a circle. Mencken (1945:615-16) cites and gives the text of A.A. Roback's 1933 recounting of the opinion of the historian Gotthard Deutsch from c. 1910. Many Russian Jewish immigrants, even before they learned English, became drummers. They reportedly used a traditional system of circles or *kikels* for the keeping of accounts. Such a drummer became known as a *kike*. Mencken (p. 616) also noted that after World War I *kike* acquired an extended meaning to apply to any Jew in ill favor. This perhaps only reflected its earlier use as a general status derogation among Jews.

Rosten (1968:182-84) reviews all the stories and underscores as most likely a derivation from *kikel*. Rosten puzzles over how *kike* could have made the transition from the German *kieken*, the Scottish and North Country *keek*, or the Yiddish version *kick*. Rosten also rejects the Lacher story, noting that "the letters *ski* or *sky* were always pronounced *skee*, and repetition-play would surely have given the neologism 'kee-kees,' or 'keeks,' not *kikes*." Rosten favors a better documented version of the origin from *kikel*, a circle. He concludes that *kike* was "born" on Ellis Island, citing a letter from Sidney Berry, who related the observation of Philip Cowen, "dean of immigration inspectors" at Ellis Island, later the founder and first editor of *The American Hebrew*. Jewish immigrants, some of whom were illiterate or were not familiar with the Roman-English alphabet, refused to make their mark with the customary "X," which represented to them the sign of the cross, under which they have been persecuted; instead they made a circle, a *kikel*. "Before long," says Rosten, "the immigration inspectors were calling anyone who signed with an 'O' instead of an 'X' a *kikel* or *kikeleh* or *kikee* or, finally and succinctly, *kike*." Rosten also accepts the related story that back-country drummers and, he adds, merchants on the Lower East Side of New York, also probably for religious reasons, kept their accounts with a *kikeleh*, a little circle, and became known as *kike-men* or *kikes*.

Scholarly opinion then is of at least three minds. Tamony (1977) favors a basic etymology from *keek*, reinforced with coincidental sounds and associations, though he does not deal with or even mention the competing etymology from *kikel*. *Webster's Third* says that it is probably from a reduplication of *-ki*. Juxtaposed with two spongy stories, which generallly lack corroborative evidence, Rosten (1968) makes a cogent case that *kike* is from *kikel*. It sounds folklorish that *kike* was "born" on Ellis Island, but the basic explanation of the story rings true. An etymology of any certainty remains to be established. Nonetheless, all the stories suggest that the term arose from within Jewish-American culture and society and then became used by outsiders as a generic nickname for Jews.

OFAY

Ofay is a black term for whites, having early Southern rural use and later vigorous use in the urban North. *Ofay* also appears in the playful variant *ofaginzy* and in the shortened *fay*, among other variants. Its origin has been a mystery. Cassidy (1975) reviews the major American dictionaries to summarize that the more cautious say "etymology unknown" and the less cautious venture, with varying degrees of confidence, the popular belief that it is Pig Latin for "foe." The especially urban idea of all whites as the enemy—the "foe"—may have reinforced this story.

Beyond this fancy has had free reign. It has been said that *ofay* may be reinforced by the sound of *oaf*. It has also been suggested that the shortened form *fay* is reinforced by the identical slang word for a male homosexual; this would be a theme of sexual insult that occurs in other black terms for whites, specifically, *queer* and *faggit*. (Also cf. *fey* in the sense of "strange.") Usually discredited (e.g., Flexner 1976), is the associative etymology that *ofay* derives from French *au lait* and, presumably, from an image of milk-whitened coffee. There is even a story that it derives from French *au fait*—a closer coincidence of sound but fantastic. The trouble with all these stories is that they sound literary and like ex post facto imaginings. They "smell of the lamp."

Cassidy (1975) puts forth the fetching possibility that *ofay* is a survival of the Yoruba *ófę́* , which signifies a magical power of instant disappearance or transportation to another place, especially when a more powerful, unbeatable enemy is in sight. He reports that the belief of magical transportation is still recalled in Jamaica, though there is no evidence· of *ofay* or *ófę́* in the dialect. Cassidy concludes, "That this word could have been brought to the United States by slaves is altogether possible. Speakers of Yoruba and related languages were numerous among Nigerians transported to the American colonies. The Negroes' practice of putting on a mask of 'know-nothing' at the approach of bosses or other whites as the better part of caution is well known. Thus *ofay* may be taken as a word said for self-protection in times of threat, which was then transferred to the source of threat, and so came to mean 'white man.'" Cassidy's story hangs together and, if true, it is richly based on the black experience. If this is not the origin, then *ofay* should be returned to "etymology unknown."

HONKY

Honky, sometimes spelled *honkey* or *honkie*, is among the most popular new collective terms used for whites by some blacks. Speculations abound. An immediate pitfall into folk etymology is that it has something to do with *honky-tonk*, which is highly improbable. Major (1970) says that *honky* is of Southern origin, while Landy (1971) says it originated in Harlem. Though most whites became aware of being called *honky* by blacks only in the 1960s, the term is probably decades older as *hunky*.

The most cogent etymology is that *honky* is a variant of *hunky* (sometimes spelled *hunkey or hunkie*), the term that appeared at the turn of the last century to denominate Central and East European immigrants, apparently first Hungarians (Morris and Morris 1977; Algeo 1977; Beresky 1978). *Hunky* probably derives from the first four letters of *Hungarian*, with the *g* changed to *k*. (Cf. the variants *bohunk* and *hunk*.) The wide applications of the term to several groups was possibly influenced by the American slang idea of a "hunk," a stout man. *Hunky* was quickly applied to all working-class or peasant immigrants from Central, East, and Southeast Europe and eventually to any unskilled or semiskilled workers, regardless of their regional or ethnic origins. Algeo (1977) notes how *hunky* and *bohunk* were "soon transferred to the occupation typical of east Europeans in large American cities—'factory hand,' with connotations of general obtuseness and stupidity." Weseen (1934) reported that *hunky* was a term used among hoboes and tramps for any stupid person or a dullard.

But why the mispronunciation indicated by the variant spelling? Johnson (1972) accepts the origin from *hunky* and says that the word was given special meaning and became fully a black word when it was first pronouned *honky* by Stokely Carmichael. Johnson suggests that the pronunciation is deliberately and significantly black. "The pronunciation change indicates the intensify of the hate black people have for white people. The pronunciation of the first syllable has been changed to conform to the prounciation given to the word 'hungry' when one is intensely hungry—hungry is to be just hungry; hongry is to be famished." That, or else *honky* is simply a black English or Southern dialectal pronunciation of *hunky*.

Two pieces of indirect evidence increase the cogency of an origin from *hunky*. First, *hunky* (not yet spelled *honky*) as a black word for all whites has been in use at least since the early 1940s when it was recorded by Carter (1944). Moseley (1971) reports the use of both *hunky* and *honky* for whites among black college students in east Texas. Second, the phenomenon of blacks borrowing a white nickname for a white minority group as a derogatory nickname for all whites has at least one other instance: the case of *paddy* (also *patty* and *paddy-boy*), another black nickname for whites. The same *paddy* (also variantly *patty*) is one of the most popular and durable nicknames for the Irish, dating from the eighteenth century. In the same way as *hunky*, *paddy* probably emerged from a nickname specifically for one group (here the Irish) to a more general term for all whites.

The *hunky*-to-*honky* story is sometimes resisted by blacks, perhaps in part because it is awkward to assimilate ideologically. Clifton (1978), for example, reports that the suggestion of this etymology was in the 1960s hooted down by a California audience of young black people. Other stories may be favored because they seem more spontaneous and independent of white culture. Here are some other imaginative speculations:

One of the most-told stories come in several variations. It is inspired by a black observation that whites do a lot of automobile horn honking. Flexner (1976) recalls but rejects the story that *honky* comes from the practice of white men calling for their black women friends by sitting in cars in front of the houses where the women worked as maids and honking their horns. Algeo (1977) also recalls the same folk etymology, with the slight variation, that white employers, in picking up black maids, use to drive to the woman's house and honk the car horn. Clifton (1978), sympathetically and imaginatively, says that the implication of *honky* "may be that such people [white liberals] honk their horns a lot, i.e., make noise, but don't actually do much about what they profess to believe. In short, a *honky* is a [white] hypocrite." But he does add that this explanation "may well be wrong."

Yet another story makes an entirely different association. It is a popular misconception that *honky* derives from the supposedly nasal tone of white speech—a "honk." In the 1960s and perhaps earlier, *honk* was a term of Eastern prep school derivation that connoted, in the words of Tom Wolfe (1968), "both the nasal quality of the upper-class voice and its presumably authoritative sound, commanding obedience, like the horn of a large 1936 Packard." A *wonk*, on the other hand, was anyone who was non-aristocratic. Wolfe notes, parenthetically, that the black word *honky* in unrelated to *honk*, and that the former "apparently" is a variation of *hunky*.

Finally, there has been at least one effort to find the roots of *honky* in an African language. Dalby (1972) ventures that *honky* may derive from the Wolof *honq*, meaning "red, pink." Dalby correctly notes that allusions to red and pink occur in other black terms for whites, such as *pink*, *pinky*, *pinktoes*, and *red-face-peck*. At least two other black nicknames for whites, *ofay* (Cassidy 1975) and *buckra* (Cassidy 1978) probably derive from African words. But the case of *honky* from *hunky*, all in all, seems most probable.

PECKERWOOD

Peckerwood, the old black term for whites, sometimes shortened to *pecker* and *peck*, is probably just the old identical Southernism for a poor white or rustic, which was used by blacks and whites alike. *Peckerwood* was originally a colloquial inverting of *woodpecker*, the common name for several species of that bird in the South. (*Hoppergrass*, dating from 1829, was formed in the same manner from *grasshopper*.) In some way, probably in the nineteenth century, the jocular, colloquial name for a bird became a derisive nickname for a poor white. Flexner (1976:58) says that *peckerwood*, as a black term for whites, originated in the 1930s to mean "a poor rural White, a lazy, ignorant rustic....Though originally White use, in Alabama, Blacks have used the word often in referring to poor Southern Whites." *Peckerwood*, as a black term for whites, is almost certainly a white class epithet that was borrowed and turned on whites generally in a way similar to *honky* and other terms.

Folk etymologies of *peckerwood*, predictably, turn the story around a little to have it originate with blacks and make an observation about poor whites. Johnson (1972), for example, repeats the story that *peckerwood* for whites comes from the observation that the sunburned necks of white men in the South "resembled the red necks of woodpeckers; thus 'peckerwood' was coined to refer to whites." (He says, further, and probably correctly, that the class epithet, *redneck*, originated with the same observation of the red necks of working men. *The Dictionary of American English* traces *redneck* back to at least 1830, though it does not define it.) The meaning for *peckerwood* or poor white Southerner is probably of more recent origin, early in this century, though it was not widely known until the Great Depression. Apparently, both *peckerwood* and *redneck*, as white *and* black nicknames for poor white Southerners, became widely known in the 1930s. Yet Major

(1970) hints that *peckerwood* is of black origin. "The word," he writes, "came into use as a result of the vivid presence in the South of red woodpecking birds that black people saw as a symbol of whites; on the other hand, they saw the common black bird as a symbol of themselves. The word was turned around to preserve the privacy of its meaning and origin."

CANUCK

Canuck, the derogatory nickname for a French Canadian in the United States, is of greatly disputed origin. Avis (1967) says that in Canada "it is probable that the term first designated a French Canadian since in the early nineteenth century the term *Canadian* itself most often referred to a French Canadian." Despite a popular misconception, when used within Canada today the term is not considered offensive, and it is not directed at Franco-Canadians in particular. Rather, it is a nickname of neutral affect used for any Canadian or for Canadians in general (e.g., Avis 1967). There is a hockey team named the Vancouver "Canucks."

Pierre Elliott Trudeau (1977), in a letter to the *New York Times*, respond-ing to a request to comment on a dispute generated by William Safire's (1976) breezy use of *canuck* for "Canadians," writes: "Personally, I have never heard it used pejoratively in connection with French Canadians, nor have I heard or read the term being used by the French Canadians."

Nevertheless, in the United States it is clearly a derogatory nickname for the French-speaking immigrants from Quebec. In the Presidential primaries of 1972, the Nixon "dirty tricks" campaign planted a rumor that Senator Edward Muskie had used the term, which caused him brief embarrassment and prompted a vigorous denial (Safire 1978:97-98).

The origin of *canuck* is highly uncertain. *The Random House Dictionary* says simply that it derives from *Can*(ada) + *uck*, the second syllable being of unknown origin. *Webster's Third* says just that it is probably an alteration of *Canadian*. Mathews (1975) recalls various speculations that it is an Indian word, that it is from the surname *Connaught* ("at first used by the Canadian French of the Irish among them"), and that endings such as *-uc*, *-oc*, or *-uck* had been added to *Can*(ada). Flexner (1976:378) also says that *canuck* may come from *Connaught*, or that it could be an Indian pronun-ciation of *Canadian*. Others merely associate the nickname with "Jack

Canuck" or "Johnny Canuck," the nineteenth-century national symbol like John Bull or Uncle Sam. But this does not explain where Johnny or Jack got his surname, *Canuck*.

The most probable origin of *canuck* is by far the most colorful story and reaches deeply into Canadian and New England history. The emergence of *canuck* involves early nineteenth-century whalers' slang for South Sea Islanders, the whaling ports in Hawaii, diffusion by returning whalers back to Canada and New England, and the importation into Canada of Sandwich Islanders to work as canoemen in the fur trade. A reader could turn to Adler (1975), Mathews (1975), and Sledd (1978) for interesting details. Mathews (1975) writes that "It is clearly a shortened form of *Kanacka*, which is the Hawaiian word for 'man,'" and he shows how the word may have gone through several spellings changes. Sledd (1978) amplifies this etymology, traces the term to the early nineteenth century, and adds that it probably came through the French *canaque*. "It is my conjecture," writes Sledd, "that the epithet *Canuck* is Hawaiian *kanacka* in French dress as *canaque* and that it was first applied to French Canadian canoemen, and later to all French Canadians, as an expression of contempt like that in which the British and the Yankees held the indentured Sandwich Islanders." While this may seem a distant connection, other ethnic nicknames may have traveled in a similar way to attach to remote groups, such as *guinea* for Italians.

GRINGO

Gringo has passed, mainly by way of Latin American Spanish, into American (and British) slang. In Latin American Spanish, *gringo* means a foreigner or particularly an English-speaking person, usually North American (cf. Spanish *Yanqui*). In Argentina, it was said to apply to all foreigners. North Americans (and the English) now apply it to themselves humorously or ironically to indicate various relations, as foreigners, vis-à-vis Latin Americans. There is wide and long scholarly agreement that *gringo* originated in Spain in the early seventeenth century as an alteration of the colloquial Spanish *griego*, Greek (e.g., Vizetelly 1929; Fuson 1961; Paredes 1961; Ronan 1964; Schmiedel 1978). Later it came to mean "gibberish" spoken, or Spanish badly spoken, by foreigners—about any foreigner—much as we say, "That's Greek to me."

The interests that wish to ameliorate cultural relations between North and South, I suspect, have been in some part resonsible for the otherwise inexplicable persistence of stories that *gringo* derives from culture contact in the Mexican War of 1847. The most popular variation has the Mexicans overhearing the American invasion troops singing Robert Burns's song whose title and first line went, "Green grow the rashes, O" The Mexicans supposedly corrupted the sound of the first two words of the line to *gringo*. A second version has it that the U.S. Marines participating in the invasion wore green coats. So the Mexicans inexplicably referred to them in English as "green coats," which they corrupted to *gringos*. Fuson (1961) recounts yet other folk etymologies.

These certainly spurious anecdotes pop up every now and then (e.g., Morgan 1977), and even appear as a quasi-official explanation for tourists ("the two most accepted theories") in an English-language publication (*Guide Magazine* 1981) placed in rooms of large hotels in Mexico City. These precious stories are sometimes accompanied by an insistence that North Americans should take no offense when they are called *gringo* or *gringa*, because the term is not usually meant to be derogatory. But it is well-known that usually it is to some degree pejorative, certainly more than *anglo* but less than *gabacho*, two other terms that denominate Americans.

But speculation persists. Holt (1961) agrees that the explanations from "Green grow the rashes, O" and "green coats" are probably fantastic, and he largely accepts the origin from *griego*, yet he goes on to write:

Another possibly decidely worth considering is the Ringgold theory. The name (now familiar as that of an army post in Texas, and of other places in the South and West) was borne by Major Samuel Ringgold, a conspicuously gallant officer under General Zachary Taylor in the Mexican War. He was mortally wounded in the battle of Palo Alto (1846), but he had already become a veritable bogeyman to Mexican marauders, particularly through his development of a flying artillery corps. Incidentally, his brother, Cadwallader Ringgold, was in 1824 an officer in Commodore Porter's West Indies fleet. And OED's earliest quotation for *gringo* is 1844. By trilling the *r* of Ringgold and omitting the final consonants, as a Mexican would tend to do, we get something quite like *gringo*. Further, it seems possible that the border peons would be more familiar with the dreaded name of Ringgold than with the Castilian slang for "foreigner."

If that is not enough, Paredes (1961:289) tells us the latest folk etymology he had heard about "the Mexican who comes to the United States and is caught in downtown traffic. The lights say, 'Red *stop*; green *go*.' So he calls Americans *gringos* because they go on green."

CONCLUDING REMARKS

Folk etymologies of well-known nicknames for ethnic groups can sometimes be interpreted as ideology. Some of the stories are clearly allegories or parables of intergroup relations, whose actors are metaphors for ingroups and outgroups. Whether people have identified positively or negatively with the victims, or with the victimizers, may influence which specious story is embraced and how it is subsequently embellished. The most probable etymology determined by scholars is sometimes more evocative of rich, historical group experience than the folk etymological versions.

I note three propensities in folk etymologies. First, the most probable etymology, which also tells a story, usually indicates that the nickname derives from historical conflict centering especially on ethnic migrations, rather than from isolated events or wry observations on the appearance and habits of an outgroup. Second, I am impressed with how often nicknames are in fact borrowed from the group that originated the term. This usually occurs when an ingroup term of status derogation is borrowed by outsiders to derogate the whole group. Third, the nickname for a greatly despised group, often a racial minority, is sometimes used for a less despised minority that may not be a racial minority, as in the cases of *canuck* and *guinea*. The same occurs for other nicknames whose origins are not disputed.

The observations throughout this book on how nicknames originate in interethnic conflict also alert us to the ways in which nicknames are not likely to originate. Fanciful associations, particularly coincidences of sound and bookish allusions, are frequently ex post facto imaginings. Stories whose point is a shrewd or humorous observation about the foibles of the target group are often fabrications. Stories that neutralize or sterilize a nickname, as with a precious anecdote, may have been perpetuated to improve the image or reduce the embarassment of the name-callers. Finally, stories that express moral indignation about the treatment of a minority at the hands of a majority are sometimes usefully regarded as parables that reflect minority-group outrage.

CHAPTER 7 **AFTERWORD**

The lexical data presented in this study bear out, to my satisfaction, the summary propositions at the end of chapter 2. The historical inventory of ordinary ethnic epithets in American English chronicles social organization and change in an ethnically diverse America. More generally, the aggregate of these words is a remarkable example of the reflection of society in language, revealing images of ethnic America through the eyes of those who were in the fray. A sociological analysis of these words, which are too often regarded only for the prejudices they reflect, enlarges our understanding of their social origins in the rough and tumble of a diverse, especially urban society.

In the context of the sociology of intergroup relations, this study gives additional support to the idea that subjective ethnocentrism and prejudice grow out of objective situations that produce and reproduce conflict among groups. The lexical data show once again that ethnocentrism, which rationalizes and guides conflict, emerges when and where groups meet and struggle. Some of the old words are kept alive—and new ones invented—to the extent that they serve conflict today.

Many of the words, and the folk etymologies of several, are part of the urban folklore of ethnicity. As such, they are weapons of the ideologies of ethnic relations. For majorities, name-calling justifies inequality and discrimination by sanctioning invidious cultural comparisons in order to produce and maintain social class and ethnic privilege. For minorities, name-calling redresses social injustice and dignifies an imposed minority status.

I have construed the data to suggest that ethnic conflict is part and parcel of the more general social process of stratifying the local community and the nation. This activity, so richly expressed in nicknames for outgroups, includes relegation of newcomers to low status, efforts of high-ranking groups to maintain the order that ever threatens to change, pushing and shoving by groups in the middle to gain advantage over their equals and to maintain it over lower-ranking groups, and redressing by minority groups of their low status. Within groups, persons are called names to rank them with respect to their conformity to core values of the group.

The eminent dialectologist, Raven I. McDavid, Jr. (1979:9), about forty years ago wrote, "Lexical research is not so much linguistic research as research in the culture of a community." Lexical research, I will add, also can be research in the social organization of a community. One of the more engaging jobs sociologists have is to study the interplay between the ordinary stuff of everyday life, such as popular speech, and the organization of society itself.

APPENDIX A **EXCLUDED CLASSES**
OF RELATED NICKNAMES

What sort of people do you have out there?—Waal, we've got some o' most all kinds: Pukes, Wolverines, Snags, Hoosiers, Griddle-greasers, Buck-eyes, Corn-crackers, Pot-soppers, Hard-heads, Hawk-eyes, Rackensacks, Linsey-woolseys, Red-horses, Mud-heads, Green-horns, Canada Patriots, Loafers, Masons, Anti-Masons, Mormons, and some few from the Jarseys.—William Irving Paulding, from *American Comedies*, 1847, p. 192

Chapter 3 lists only those nicknames that meet the criterion of a nounal epithet for persons of a specific ethnic outgroup. Several related classes of terms also denote or connote ethnicity and might seem obvious candidates for the lexicon. But for various reasons these terms do not meet the criterion and are excluded.

Ethnicity in American life is also displayed in lexical inventories that are not terms for specific ethnic groups, such as political epithets and nicknames for residents of particular states. While the targets sometimes are coincidentally persons of a particular ethnicity, their ethnicity was not the target of the nicknames. Such political epithets are excluded from the study and from the lists in chapter 3. Also excluded are terms of general xenophobia, proposed but unaccepted proper names for ethnic groups, and many words that have ethnic references but are either too oblique or too specific to include as generic nicknames. But each of these classes of names is related to, and is likely to be confused with, terms for specific groups. For these reasons each class warrants a brief description in order to distinguish between included and excluded classes of terms.

I have omitted many, probably more than a hundred, eighteenth- and nineteenth-century terms for North American political and regional factions, which were sometimes composed almost entirely of a particular ethnic group, such as the city Irish, the colonial Dutch or English, or the Scotch-Irish in the South. But politics rather than ethnicity was the primary referent of these terms. Similarly, in the Revolutionary War, the War of 1812, and the Civil War many nicknames appeared for soldiers and sympathizers with related political causes. For example, *Blue-lights* was applied to New England Federalists who opposed the War of 1812.

I have excluded political epithets for foreign political entities that are sometimes coincidental with ethnic entities, such as the blend *chicom* for the people of the People's Republic of China. Again, the nicknames were not ethnically aimed and, unlike many of the names spawned by foreign wars (e.g., *Nazi* for Germans), they were not subsequently applied to counterpart ethnic groups living in this country.

I have, for the most part, omitted another large group of words that sometimes connote ethnicity. Perhaps a hundred nicknames were applied to residents of particular states in the United States. These terms were especially popular in the nineteenth century, when most were coined (e.g., Mencken 1949). Many of these nicknames were meant to be derogatory; a number are derisive animal metaphors. Others derive from things, activities, historical events, and products assorted with particular states. As a class of nicknames, they semantically resemble terms for ethnic groups. A few of these words either originally were, or subsequently became, nicknames for ethnic groups and are, for those reasons, included in the study. *Cracker*, for an elaborate example, started as a nickname for certain Scotch-Irish, attached to any resident of Georgia, and then reemerged as an ethnic epithet for Southerners in general.

In general, former and proposed proper names for groups have not been included. However, *colored* is included because it has never been in good repute and *black* is included because it was used as an epithet before the late 1960s (Robbins 1949). Proposed proper names for blacks are not included, such as *Africo-American* [1835],· *Aframerican, African, Raceman* [1936], and others. *Afro-American* [1880], revived briefly in the 1960s, is used in chapter 3 to title the list of terms for blacks. *Amerindian* [1889], later shortened to *Amerind, Natam* [1970s], and *Filamerican* are excluded. Proper names once accepted but now being rejected by some in the referent group as inappropriate or variously offensive are not included as nicknames, such as *Indian, Eskimo, Mexican-American, French Canadian*, and others.

I have excluded all xenophobic names used by certain groups for all outgroups. Gypsies call non-Gypsies *gadjo* [fem. *gadji*, plural *gadjé*]. Jews sometimes call non-Jews *gentiles*, and a shortened form, *'tiles*, has had some recent campus use. (The Mormons also use *gentile* for anyone who is not Mormon or Jewish. Farmer [1889] said it was "amongst Mormons, a contemptuous epithet.") In Yiddish, a non-Jew is a *goy* [plural, *goyim*] from the Hebrew *goy*, nation. A young woman is a *shikseh* and a young man, a *shaygets*. Both terms are derogatory in their etymologies but today tend to be jocular. *Goy* and *shikseh* have entered the mainstream of American slang, as in *goy-boy*, and usually they are used with irony. Even a back-slang form, *yog*, has been listed.

A related class of excluded terms is used by particular groups to name other broad categories of outsiders with whom historically they have been in conflict. Mexicans have several variously derogatory terms for, especially, white Anglophones from north of the border. The most derogating term is probably *gabacho*, meaning "frog," "frenchy," "foreigner," which is not yet widely known among Anglophones. *Bolillo, güero*, and *chicas-patas* are even less known (Paredes 1961). Less derogating and more familiar is *gringo*, which is a very old word originally applied to any foreigner who spoke Spanish badly or not at all (see chapter 6). *Anglo*, from the combining form *Anglo-* (English), has been used since 1941 as a noun and is mildly derogating. Nonetheless, it recently has had wide use in the American press and academic writing. More widely in Latin America, *yanqui* has been used since the early nineteenth century, though North Americans did not learn it until the 1950s from the phrase, "Yanqui, go home" (Flexner 1976:322).

There are other terms of the same order used by other groups. Hawaiian *haole*, stranger, literally "no breath," is a non-Hawaiian, especially a white U.S. mainlander. *Roundeye* has been used for white Americans by American groups of various Asian backgrounds, I suspect jocularly, as a comeback for *slanteye*. *White-eye* is reportedly another, I suspect, recent, American Indian term for any white, but I do not understand the allusion, unless it is a combination of *white* and *round-eye*. *Paleface* [1822] is not of Native Indian invention; James Fenimore Cooper put it in the mouths of his Indian characters. *Paleman* [1808], on the other hand, may be a genuine American Indian term for any white. *Long-knives* [1784] or *big-knives*, which are translations of various American Indian words, were terms for whites that originally alluded to the swords of soldiers who fought the Indians. In Canada, *kabloona* or *kabluna* [1744] and their English equivalents, *big-eyebrow*, shortened to *eyebrow*, were Native terms for a white man.

Finally, I excluded certain terms that are sometimes used with mild derogation yet are not really nicknames for ethnic groups. Adjectives when used as nouns seem to be derogative—*ethnic* when used as a code for blue-collar Catholic groups, *Hispanic* and *Latino* when used to stereotype the interests of all Latin American immigrant groups, *Appalachian* when used for any Southerner from the hill country, and *born-again* when used to reprove the emphasis on personal salvation among some evangelical Protestants. (The use of *Anglo* was mentioned above.)

I have excluded media and academic codewords for low-income blacks and other minorities, such as *inner-city youth, urban-youth, urban-poor, nonwhite, the-disadvantaged,* the *under-class, culturally-deprived,* and other jargon. *New Yorker* and *city-boy* are sometimes transparent codewords for Jews but are excluded. I have also excluded those euphemistic phrases that old immigrants used to describe new immigrants, such as *hyphenated-American* and *one-of-those-names-that-end-in-a-vowel,* and other such things.

APPENDIX B **ANNOTATIONS**

The word list in chapter 3 is briefly annotated to clarify the allusions, set the terms in historical and social context, and show available dates, gender, and remote etymologies. I do not explain allusions that are obvious to me and, I presume, to anyone generally familiar with American idioms, folklore, and popular culture. Most nicknames are clear references to physical differences, ethnic foods, personal names thought common in the groups, putative national character, transparent wordplays on the proper names of the groups, and a multitude of other familiar symbols.

Etymologies. Etymologies are indicated with surety only when there is a published source. I have not documented etymologies with citations, except for a few key, unusual, or disputed items. Almost all the origins can be verified by checking the major sources, such as Wentworth and Flexner (1975) or the unabridged dictionaries. Very few of my speculations are included, and they are confessed as they appear. I have also ignored the worst indulgences of speculation by others. Spurious etymologies are rife in older and in some of the newer but peripheral sources. The most familiar nicknames sometimes have folk etymologies, and I have examined these as a separate topic in chapter 6. In the word list, I report only authoritative etymologies that have not been challenged with equal authority. For a few items, I show two or more competing etymologies when there seems to be no strong reason to accept any one of them. Depending on their degree of plausibility, some etymologies are indicated by either "perhaps" or "probably."

Variants. The subordination of most, but not all, variants of a full entry serves both to display more compactly the variety of basic stereotypical images of groups and to preserve the full record of lexical variation. Full entries are listed in boldface between semicolons. Most variants of full entries are listed in italics between brackets with other annotative material.

I also have excluded from full entry all variant spellings, most diminutive forms, and most shortened forms. In some cases, a variant has become important in its own right and is entered as a separate item. I have excluded from full entry most variants that appear as compound phrases with added adjectival components. In a few cases, I have grouped under the main entry etymologically unrelated terms with similar themes when I decided that they were much less used or possibly nonce words.

Loan Words. Many terms for ethnic groups in languages other than English spoken in America at various times in history have entered both formal and informal American English. Some of these terms are loans from the languages of the indigenous peoples. The altogether foreign words came with foreign influences, usually immigrations. Many old words are from Dutch, German, Spanish, French, and various West African languages. Then came the words from Italian, Polish, Czech, Yiddish, and most recently a new wave of words from Latin American Spanish. European wars brought words from German, and adventures in the Pacific brought a few from Japanese and other Asian languages. Some loanwords seep into English with their original spellings and meanings intact. Others are anglicized and given variant meanings, while some are altered almost beyond recognition. I have indicated the origins of loanwords that I could identify from the sources. Etymology is a complicated and technical field, and loanwords come into a language in highly roundabout ways. In this regard I have, as a layman, brushed with many possibilities for error.

Gender. Many nicknames have overt or implied gender referents. The ethnic nickname has in large part been a male phenomenon, expressing male anxieties and conflicts, especially those of competition and rivalry in the workplace. Most names were directed principally at the men of outgroups, though most are not gender specific. I have not speculated in print whether the words were usually inclusive of both men and women or were limited only to men. About half of the terms specific of gender are feminine; many are not obvious, so all are marked *fem*. Feminine variants are counted as separate items because they, unlike most specifically masculine terms, often attach sexual insult to ethnic derogation. This gives them a singular importance, which as a result increases the inventory of basic terms.

Pejoration. All nicknames for ethnic groups represent an effort to diminish the status of an outgroup, sometimes simply by rhetorical force. Pejoration is often accomplished—or increased—by the use of suffixes and modifiers. One morphemic element with an unfavorable connotation is the suffix *-ess* to make a name feminine, such as *jewess, mulatress, negress,* and *patess.* This device also suggests an animal metaphor, since the same suffix is often used to feminize the names of feline species.

In English, names are often made diminutive witrh the endings *-y* or *-ie,* which connote small size, youth, familiarity, or affection. Traditional nicknames for persons often use these endings, such as *Jimmy* or *Suzie.* Similarly, scores of nicknames for ethnic groups terminate in *-y* or *-ie.* In nonethnic usage, the ending *-y* usually predominates over *-ie,* except when usage is clearly against it; *-ie* is often the singular termination for words usually used in the plural; and in personal nicknames, *-ie* is often considered more feminine. But I saw none of these patterns among ethnic nicknames. About half ended in *-y* and about half in *-ie.*

Other Conventions. Users of the list in chapter 3 will be helped by a brief explanation of my other conventions, which vary from those of most dictionaries. First of all, terms are not labeled "obsolescent" or "obsolete," because the fact that they were current for a time in the past is the criterion of inclusion, not their status today. Most of these nicknames are obsolescent to obsolete, though I am impressed with how many are still to be heard. Reader recognition of a term and impressions of its currency may be as good as any measure of its vitality.

Most ethnic nicknames occur as single words, and as nouns. Some occur as nouns qualified with adjectives, such as *white-, black-, yellow-, dirty-, stinking-, bastard-,* and *slimey-.* Compound phrases are always hyphenated to emphasize that those particular elements are usually paired. Many other compound phrases are omitted because they repeat terms already listed as one word. Some compound phrases are subordinated as variants. A few especially common ones are included as separate items.

All terms are entered in the singular, though many usually occur in the plural. If for this reason an entry sounds unnatural, then add an *s.* Entering all items in the singular avoids deciding which ones usually occur in the plural and avoids using space-consuming devices such as *(s)'s.* All nicknames for ethnic groups can and often do take the plural, which indicates that they are—and are used as—common nouns. In the strictest sense a proper noun cannot take the plural. In actual use, the initials of many terms are regularly capitalized as though proper nouns. I have seen little consistency in capitalizing the initial letter. It varies from source to source, from time to time, and with custom. These terms are not the proper names for the groups and thus they are not proper nouns, properly speaking (Algeo 1973).

Also to save space, I have not shown in the annotations page numbers for dictionaries and other such sources that are alphabetized or indexed by term. An author citation with no publication date simply means the author appears only once in the References section at the back of the book. Phrases beginning with "or" introduce alternative spellings; "also" introduces variants, cognates, and compounds not different enough to list as separate items.

REFERENCES

Abrahams, Roger D. 1970. *Positively Black*. Englewood Cliffs, N.J.: Prentice-Hall.

—— 1980. "Folklore." In S. Thernstrom et al., eds., *Harvard Encyclopedia of American Ethnic Groups*, pp. 370-79. Cambridge: Belknap Press of Harvard University Press.

Abrahams, Roger D. and Susan Kalčik. 1978. "Folklore and Cultural Pluralism." In R.M. Dorson, ed., *Folklore in the Modern World*, pp. 223-36. The Hague: Mouton.

Abramson, Harold J. 1973. *Ethnic Diversity in Catholic America*. New York: Wiley.

Adler, Jacob. 1975. "The Etymology of Canuck." *American Speech*, 50(Spring-Summer):158-59.

Algeo, John. 1973. *On Defining the Proper Name*. Gainesville: University of Florida Press.

—— 1977. "Xenophobic Ethnica." *Maledicta*, 1(Winter):133-40.

Allen, Harold B. 1958. "Pejorative Terms for Midwest Farmers." *American Speech*, 33(December):260-65.

Anderson, Charles H. 1970. *White Protestant Americans: From National Origins to Religious Group*. Englewood Cliffs, N.J.: Prentice-Hall.

Antoun, Richard T. 1968. "On the Significance of Names in an Arab Village." *Ethnology*, 7(April):158-70.

Appel, John J. 1963. " 'Betzemer': A Nineteenth-Century Cognomen for the Irish." *American Speech*, 38(December):307-8.

Avis, Walter S. 1967. *A Dictionary of Canadianisms on Historical Principles*. Toronto: W.J. Gage.

Bartlett, John Russell. 1877. *Dictionary of Americanisms: A Glossary of Words and Phrases Usually Regarded as Peculiar to the United States*. 4th ed. Boston: Little, Brown.

Bauman, Richard. 1972. "Differential Identity and the Social Base of Folklore." In A. Paredes and R. Bauman, eds., *Toward New Perspectives in Folklore*, pp. 31-41. Austin: University of Texas Press.

Bayor, Ronald H. 1978. *Neighbors in Conflict: The Irish, Germans, Jews, and Italians of New York City, 1929-1941*. Baltimore: Johns Hopkins University Press.

Bennett, Lerone, Jr. 1969. "What's In A Name? Negro vs. Afro-American vs. Black." *ETC: A Review of General Semantics*, 26(December):399-412.

Beresky, Andrew E. 1978. "Bleep that Slur!" *Verbatim*, 4(February):4.

Bernard, Jesse. 1951. "The Conceptualization of Intergroup Relations with Special Reference to Conflict." *Social Forces*, 29(March):243-51.

Berrey, Lester V. and Melvin Van Den Bark. 1953. *The American Thesaurus of Slang: A Complete Reference Book of Colloquial Speech*. 2d ed. [1st ed., 1942; with supplement, 1947]. New York: Thomas Y. Crowell.

Berry, Brewton. 1963. *Almost White*. New York: Macmillan.

Birmingham, Stephen. 1967. *Our Crowd: The Great Jewish Families of New York*. New York: Harper & Row.

Blalock, Hubert M., Jr. 1967. *Toward a Theory of Minority-Group Relations*. New York: Wiley.

Blau, Peter M. 1977. *Inequality and Heterogeneity: A Primitive Theory of Social Structure*. New York: Free Press.

Bradley, Francis W. 1964. "Sandlappers and Clay Eaters." *North Carolina Folklore*, 12(December):27-28.

Brearley, H.C. 1973. "Ba—ad Nigger." In Alan Dundes, ed., *Mother Wit from the Laughing Barrel*, pp. 578-85. Englewood Cliffs, N.J.: Prentice-Hall.

Burchfield, Robert. 1980. "Dictionaries and Ethnic Sensibilities." In L. Michaels and C. Ricks, eds., *The State of the Language*, pp. 15-23. Berkeley: University of California Press.

Burke, W.J. 1939. *The Literature of Slang*. New York: New York Public Library [rpt. 1965, Detroit: Gale Research].

Cahan, Abraham. 1917. *The Rise of David Levinsky*. New York: Harper.

Carter, Wilmoth A. 1944. "Nicknames and Minority Groups." *Phylon*, 5 (Third Quarter):241-45.

Cassidy, Frederick G. 1975. Communication under "Of Matters Lexicographical." *American Speech*, 50(Spring-Summer):87-89.

—— 1978. "Another Look at Buckaroo." *American Speech*, 53(Spring): 49-51.

—— Forthcoming. *Dictionary of American Regional English*. Cambridge: Belknap Press of Harvard University Press.

Claerbaut, David. 1972. *Black Jargon in White America.* Grand Rapids, Mich.: William B. Eerdmans.

Clapin, Sylva. 1902. A *New Dictionary of Americanisms: Being a Glossary of Words Supposed to Be Peculiar to the United States and the Dominion of Canada.* New York: Louis Weiss [rpt. 1968, Detroit: Gale Research.]

Clifton, Merritt. 1978. "How to Hate Thy Neighbor: A Guide to Racist Maledicta." *Maledicta,* 2(Summer-Winter):149-74.

Cohen, David Steven. 1972. "The Origin of the 'Jackson Whites': History and Legend among the Ramapo Mountain People." *Journal of American Folklore,* 85(July-September):260-66.

Colombo, John Robert. 1979. "Canadian Slurs, Ethnic and Others." *Maledicta,* 3(Winter):182-84.

Coombs, Orde. 1978. "Mulatto Pride." *New York,* June 26, pp. 33-37.

Coser, Lewis A. 1956. *The Functions of Social Conflict.* Glencoe: Free Press.

Cox, Oliver C. 1949. *Caste, Class, and Race: A Study in Social Dynamics.* Garden City, N.Y.: Doubleday.

Craigie, William A. and James R. Hulbert, eds. 1938-1944. A *Dictionary of American English on Historical Principles.* 4 vols. Chicago: University of Chicago Press.

Cray, Ed. 1962. "Ethnic and Place Names as Derisive Adjectives." *Western Folklore,* 21(January):27-34.

—— 1965. "More Ethnic and Place Names as Derisive Adjectives." *Western Folklore,* 24(July):197-98.

Dahlskog, Helen, ed. 1972. A *Dictionary of Contemporary and Colloquial Usage.* Chicago: English-Language Institute of America.

Dalby, David. 1972. "The African Element in American English." In T. Kochman, ed., *Rappin' and Stylin' Out,* pp. 170-86. Urbana: University of Illinois Press.

Dean, Florine. 1971. "Names Viewed Through the Racial Looking Glass." In F. Tarpley and A. Moseley, eds., *Of Edsels and Maurauders,* pp. 40-42. Commerce, Texas: Names Institute Press.

De Vere, Schele M. 1872. *Americanisms: The English of the New World.* New York: Charles Scribner [rpt. 1968, New York: Johnson Reprint Corporation].

Dillard, J.L. 1976. *Black Names.* The Hague: Mouton.

—— 1977. *Lexicon of Black English.* New York: Seabury Press.

Dohan, Mary Helen. 1974. *Our Own Words.* New York: Alfred A. Knopf.

Dumas, Bethany K. and Jonathan Lighter. 1978. "Is *Slang* a Word for Linguists?" *American Speech*, 53(Spring):5-17.

Dundes, Alan. 1971. "A Study of Ethnic Slurs: The Jew and the Polack in the United States." *Journal of American Folklore*, 84(April-June):186-203.

Dundes, Alan and Carl R. Pagter. 1975. *Urban Folklore from the Paperwork Empire.* Austin: American Folklore Society.

Dunlap, A.R. and C.A. Weslager. 1947. "Trends in the Naming of Tri-Racial Mixed-Blood Groups in the Eastern United States." *American Speech*, 22(April):81-87.

Ehrlich, Howard J. 1973. *The Social Psychology of Prejudice.* New York: Wiley.

Eisiminger, Sterling. 1978. "Acronyms and Folk Etymology." *Journal of American Folklore*, 91(January-March):582-84.

—— 1979. "A Glossary of Slurs in American English." *Maledicta*, 3(Winter):153-74.

Epstein, A.L. 1959. "Linguistic Innovation and Culture on the Copperbelt." *Southwestern Journal of Anthropology*, 15:235-53.

Estabrook, Arthur H. and I.E. McDougle. 1926. *Mongrel Virginians: The Win Tribe.* Baltimore: Williams and Wilkins.

Fallows, Marjorie R. 1979. *Irish Americans: Identity and Assimilation.* Englewood Cliffs, N.J.: Prentice-Hall.

Farmer, John Stephen, ed. 1889. *Americanisms—Old and New: A Dictionary of Words, Phrases, and Colloquialisms.* London: T. Poulter [rpt. 1976, Detroit: Gale Research].

Fischer, Claude S. 1975. "Toward a Subcultural Theory of Urbanism." *American Journal of Sociology*, 80(May):1319-41.

—— 1976. *The Urban Experience.* New York: Harcourt, Brace, Jovanovich.

Fishman, Joshua A. 1972. *The Sociology of Language.* Rowley, Mass.: Newbury House.

Flexner, Stuart Berg. 1960. "Preface." In H. Wentworth and S.B. Flexner, eds., *Dictionary of American Slang*, pp. vi-xv. New York: Thomas Y. Crowell.

—— 1976. *I Hear America Talking.* New York: Van Nostrand-Reinhold.

Franklyn, Julian. 1963. *A Dictionary of Nicknames.* New York: British Book Centre.

Fuson, Robert H. 1961. "The Origin of the Word *Gringo.*" In M.C. Boatright, W.M. Hudson, and A. Maxwell, eds., *Singers and Storytellers*, pp. 282-84. Publications of the Texas Folklore Society, vol. 30. Dallas: Southern Methodist University Press.

Gelfant, Blanche Housman. 1970. *The American City Novel*. Norman: University of Oklahoma Press.

Gilbert, William Harlen, Jr. 1946. "Memorandum Concerning the Characteristics of the Larger Mixed-Blood Racial Islands of the Eastern United States." *Social Forces*, 24(May):438-47.

Glanz, Rudolf. 1964. "Jewish Names in Early American Humor." In L.S. Dawidowicz et al., eds., *For Max Weinreich on His Seventieth Birthday: Studies in Jewish Languages, Literature, and Society*, pp. 63-71. The Hague: Mouton.

—— 1966. *Jew and Irish: Historic Group Relations and Immigration*. New York: published by the author.

Gordon, Milton. 1963. *Assimilation in American Life*. New York: Oxford University Press.

Gove, Philip Babcock, ed. 1961. *Webster's Third New International Dictionary of the English Language, Unabridged*. Springfield, Mass.: G. & C. Merriam.

Greeley, Andrew M. 1974. *Ethnicity in the United States*. New York: Wiley.

Grose, Francis. 1785. *A Classical Dictionary of the Vulgar Tongue*. London: S. Hooper [3d ed., 1796, rpt. 1931, ed. Eric Partridge. London: Routledge & Kegan Paul].

Guide Magazine [Mexico, D.F.]. 1981. "Gringo." 9(January):8.

Gutman, Robert. 1966. "Demographic Trends and the Decline of Anti-Semitism." In C.H. Stember et al., *Jews in the Mind of America*, pp. 354-76. New York: Basic Books.

Hamblin, Robert L. 1962. "The Dynamics of Racial Discrimination." *Social Problems*, 10(Summer):103-21.

Hare, Nathan. 1965. *The Black Anglo-Saxons*. New York: Marzani & Munsell.

Hertzler, Joyce O. 1965. *A Sociology of Language*. New York: Random House.

Higham, John. 1963. *Strangers in the Land: Patterns of American Nativism, 1860-1925*. 2d ed. New York: Atheneum.

Holt, Alfred H. 1961. *Phrase and Word Origins: A Study of Familiar Expressions*. Rev. ed. New York: Dover.

Holt, Grace Sims. 1972. "'Inversion' in Black Communication." In T. Kochman, ed., *Rappin' and Stylin' Out*, pp. 152-59. Urbana: University of Illinois Press.

Homer, Joel. 1979. *Jargon: How to Talk to Anyone About Anything*. New York: Times Books.

Howard, Philip. 1977. *New Words for Old*. New York: Oxford University Press.

Hughes, Everett Cherrington and Helen MacGill Hughes. 1952. *Where Peoples Meet*. Glencoe: Free Press.

Hutchinson, Edward P. 1956. *Immigrants and Their Children, 1850 to 1950*. New York: Wiley.

Irwin, Godfrey. 1931. *American Tramp and Underworld Slang*. New York: Sears.

Jansen, William Hugh. 1959. "The Esoteric-Exoteric Factor in Folklore." *Fabula: Journal of Folktale Studies*, 2:205-11. [Rpt. 1965 in A. Dundes, ed., *The Study of Folklore*, pp. 43-51. Englewood Cliffs, N.J.: Prentice-Hall].

Jespersen, Otto. 1922. *Language: Its Nature, Development, and Origin*. New York: Macmillan.

Johnson, Ken. 1972. "The Vocabulary of Race." In T. Kochman, ed., *Rappin' and Stylin' Out*, pp. 140-51. Urbana: University of Illinois Press.

Kantrowitz, Nathan. 1969. "The Vocabulary of Race Relations in a Prison." *Publication of the American Dialect Society*, 51(April):23-34.

Kess, Joseph F. 1976. "Terms for Slovenes." *American Speech*, 51(Fall-Winter): 295-96.

Kessner, Thomas. 1977. *The Golden Door: Italian and Jewish Immigrant Mobility in New York City, 1880-1915*. New York: Oxford University Press.

Killian, Lewis M. 1973. *White Southerners*. New York: Random House.

Kirshenblatt-Gimblett, Barbara. 1978. "Culture Shock and Narrative Creativity." In R.M. Dorson, ed., *Folklore in the Modern World*, pp. 109-22. The Hague: Mouton.

Lacher, J.H.A. 1926. "Kike." *American Speech*, 1(March):322.

Landy, Eugene E. 1971. *The Underground Dictionary*. New York: Simon and Schuster.

Laumann, Edward O. 1973. *Bonds of Pluralism*. New York: Wiley.

Lazerwitz, Bernard. 1978. "An Estimate of a Rare Population Group: The U.S. Jewish Population." *Demography*, 15(August):389-94.

Legman, G. 1966. "On Sexual Speech and Slang." In J.S. Farmer and W.E. Henley, eds., *Dictionary of Slang & Its Analogues*, pp. xxx-xciv. Vol. 1. Rev. ed. New Hyde Park, N.Y.: University Books.

LeVine, Robert A. and Donald T. Campbell. 1972. *Ethnocentrism: Theories of Conflict, Ethnic Attitudes, and Group Behavior*. New York: Wiley.

Lipski, John M. 1976. "Prejudice and Pronunciation." *American Speech*, 51(Spring-Summer):109-18.

Lopata, Helena Znaniecki. 1976. *Polish Americans: Status Competition in an Ethnic Community*. Englewood Cliffs: Prentice-Hall.

McCarthy, Kevin M. 1970. "The Derisive Use of *Turk* and *Turkey*." *American Speech*, 45(Spring-Summer):157-59.

McDavid, Raven I., Jr. 1960. "A Study in Ethnolinguistics." *The Southern Speech Journal*, 25(Summer):247-54.

—— 1967. "Word Magic or 'Would You Want Your Daughter to Marry a Hoosier?' " *Indiana English Journal*, 2(Fall):1-7.

—— 1979. *Dialects in Culture: Essays in General Dialectology*. Ed. W.A. Kretzschmar, Jr. University: University of Alabama Press.

McDavid, Raven I., Jr. and Virginia McDavid. 1973. "Cracker and Hoosier." *Names*, 21(September):161-67.

McDavid, Raven I., Jr. and Sarah Ann Witham. 1974. "Poor Whites and Rustics." *Names*, 22(September):93-103.

McDowell, John H. 1981. "Toward a Semiotics of Nicknaming: The Kamsá Example." *Journal of American Folklore*, 94(January-March):1-18.

McLaughlin, W.A. 1914. "Some Current Substitutes for 'Irish.' " *Dialect Notes*, 4:146-48.

MacMullen, Jerry. 1963. "Derisive Ethnic Names." *Western Folklore*, 22(July):197.

Maitland, James. 1891. *The American Slang Dictionary*. Chicago: R.J. Kittredge.

Major, Clarence. 1970. *Dictionary of Afro-American Slang*. New York: International Publishers.

Mathews, Mitford M. 1951. *A Dictionary of Americanisms on Historical Principles*. 2 vols. Chicago: University of Chicago Press.

—— 1975. "The Etymology of *Canuck*." *American Speech*, 50(Spring-Summer):158-60.

Maurer, David W. 1978. "Slang." In *The New Encyclopedia Britannica*, vol. 16, pp. 850-53. Chicago: Encyclopedia Britannica.

Mayhew, Bruce H. and Roger L. Levinger. 1976. "Size and Density of Interaction in Human Aggregates." *American Journal of Sociology*, 2(July):86-110

Mencken, H.L. 1936. *The American Language*. 4th ed. New York: Alfred A. Knopf.

—— 1944. "Designations for Colored Folk." *American Speech*, 19(October):161-74.

—— 1945. *The American Language*. Supplement One. New York: Alfred A. Knopf.

—— 1949. "Some Opprobrious Nicknames." *American Speech*, 24(February):25-30.

—— 1963. *The American Language*. The 4th ed. and the two supplements, abridged, with annotations and new material, by Raven I. McDavid, Jr. With the assistance of David W. Maurer. New York: Alfred A. Knopf.

Miller, Casey and Kate Swift. 1977. *Words and Women*. Garden City: Doubleday/Anchor.

Monteiro, George. 1968. "And Still More Ethnic and Place Names as Derisive Adjectives." *Western Folklore*, 27(January):51.

Moore, Richard B. 1960. *The Name "Negro": Its Origin and Evil Uses*. New York: Argentina Press.

Morgan, Arthur J. 1977. "The Encompassing Circle." *Verbatim*, 4(May):6.

Morgan, J., C. O'Neill, and R. Harré. 1979. *Nicknames: Their Origins and Social Consequences*. London: Cambridge University Press.

Morris, William and Mary Morris. 1977. *The Morris Dictionary of Word and Phrase Origins*. New York: Harper & Row.

Moseley, Ann. 1971. "The Opposite of Black: Names for White Americans." In F. Tarpley and A. Moseley, eds., *Of Edsels and Maurauders*, pp. 33-39. Commerce, Texas: Names Institute Press.

Moskos, Charles C., Jr. 1980. *Greek Americans: Struggle and Success*. Englewood Cliffs, N.J.: Prentice-Hall.

Müller, Karl-Ludwig. 1973. *Übertragener Gebrauch von Ethnika in der Romania: Eine vergleichende Untersuchung unter Berücksichtigung der englischen und deutschen Sprache*. Meisenheim am Glan: Anton Hain.

Needler, Geoffrey D. 1967. "An Antedating of 'Nigger.' " *American Speech*, 42(May):159-60.

Newman, William M. 1973. *American Pluralism*. New York: Harper & Row.

Nichols, Edward J. 1945. *Hunky Johnny*. Boston: Houghton Mifflin.

Opie, Iona and Peter Opie. 1959. *Lore and Language of Schoolchildren*. Oxford: Oxford University Press.

Opie, Peter. 1970. "Children's Derogatory Epithets." *Journal of American Folklore*, 83(July-September):354-55.

Otto, John Solomon and Augustus M. Burns. 1972. "The Use of Race and Hillbilly Recordings as Sources for Historical Research: The Problem of Color Hierarchy among Afro-Americans in the Early Twentieth Century." *Journal of American Folklore*, 85(October-December):344-55.

Palmore, Erdman B. 1962. "Ethnophaulisms and Ethnocentrism." *American Journal of Sociology*, 67(January):442-45.

Paredes, Américo. 1961. "On *Gringo, Greaser*, and Other Neighborly Names." In M.C. Boatright, W.M. Hudson, and A. Maxwell, eds., *Singers and Storytellers*, pp. 285-90. Publications of the Texas Folklore Society, vol. 30. Dallas: Southern Methodist University Press.

Paredes, Américo and Ellen J. Stekert, eds. 1971. *The Urban Experience and Folk Tradition*. Austin: University of Texas Press.

Parrish, Charles H. 1946. "Color Names and Color Notions." *Journal of Negro Education*, 15(Winter):13-20.

Partridge, Eric. 1933. *Words, Words, Words!* London: Methuen.

—— 1970. *A Dictionary of Slang and Unconventional English*. 7th ed. New York: Macmillan.

Pederson, Lee A. 1964. "Terms of Abuse for Some Chicago Social Groups." *Publication of the American Dialect Society*, 42(November):26-48.

—— 1980. "Lexical Data from the Gulf States." *American Speech*, 55(Fall):195-203.

Porter, Kenneth. 1965 "Racism in Children's Rhymes and Sayings, Central Kansas, 1910-1918." *Western Folklore*, 24(July):191-96.

—— 1966. "Still More Ethnic and Place Names as Derisive Adjectives." *Western Folklore*, 25(January):37-40.

—— 1967. "More and Still More Ethnic and Place Names as Derisive and Jocular Adjectives." *Western Folklore*, 26(July):189-91.

Presley, Delma E. 1976. "The Crackers of Georgia." *The Georgia Historical Quarterly*, 60(Summer):102-16.

Price, Charles H. 1980. "Methods of Estimating the Size of Groups." In S. Thernstrom et al., eds., *Harvard Encyclopedia of American Ethnic Groups*, pp. 1033-44. Cambridge: Belknap Press of Harvard University Press.

Reed, John Shelton. 1973. *The Enduring South*. Lexington: D.C. Heath.

Revens, Lee. 1966. "Introduction." In J.S. Farmer and W.E. Henley, eds., *Dictionary of Slang and Its Analogues*, pp. vii-xxix. Vol. 1, rev. ed. New Hyde Park, N.Y.: University Books.

Roback, A.A. 1944. *A Dictionary of International Slurs*. Cambridge: Sci-Art Publishers [rpt. 1979, Waukesha, Wisconsin: Maledicta Press].

Robbins, Rossel Hope. 1949. "Social Awareness and Semantic Change." *American Speech*, 24(April):156-58.

Roberts, Hermese E. 1971. *The Third Ear: A Black Glossary*. Chicago: English Language Institute of America.

Ronan, Charles E. 1964. "Observations on the Word *Gringo.*" *Arizona and the West*, 6(Spring):23-29.

Rosten, Leo. 1968. *The Joys of Yiddish.* New York: Penguin.

Safire, William. 1976. "54-40 and No Fight." *New York Times*, November 22, p. A-25.

—— 1978. *Safire's Political Dictionary.* 3d ed. New York: Ballantine Books.

Sagarin, Edward. 1962. *The Anatomy of Dirty Words.* New York: Lyle Stuart.

Schell, Ruth. 1963. "Swamp Yankee." *American Speech*, 35(May):121-23.

Schermerhorn, R.A. 1970. *Comparative Ethnic Relations: A Framework for Theory and Research.* New York: Random House.

Schmiedel, Donald E. 1978. Untitled communication under "Epistolae." *Verbatim*, 5(May):19.

Schulman, J. Frank. 1977. "The Sinister Side of the Language." *Verbatim*, 4(May):4.

Schulz, Muriel R. 1975. "The Semantic Derogation of Woman." In B. Thorne and N. Henley, eds., *Language and Sex*, pp. 64-75. Rowley, Mass.: Newbury House.

Seago, Dorothy W. 1947. "Stereotypes: Before Pearl Harbor and After." *The Journal of Psychology*, 23(1):55-63.

Simmel, Georg. 1904. "Sociology of Conflict (Part I)." *American Journal of Sociology*, 9:490-525.

Simmons, Donald C. 1966. "Anti-Italian American Riddles in New England." *Journal of American Folklore*, 79(July-Sept.):475-78.

Simpson, George Eaton and J. Milton Yinger. 1965. *Racial and Cultural Minorities: An Analysis of Prejudice and Discrimination.* 3d ed. New York: Harper & Row.

Sledd, James. 1978. "What are We Going to Do about It Now That We're Number One?" *American Speech*, 53(Fall):171-98.

Spears, Richard A. 1981. *Slang and Euphemism.* Middle Village, N.Y.: Jonathan David Publishers.

Spoehr, Luther W. 1973. "Sambo and the Heathen Chinee: California's Racial Stereotypes in the Late 1870's." *Pacific Historical Review*, 42(May):185-204.

Stack, John F., Jr. 1979. *International Conflict in an American City: Boston's Irish, Italians, and Jews, 1935-44.* Westport, Conn.: Greenwood Press.

Stein, Jess and Laurence Urdang, eds. 1966. *The Random House Dictionary of the English Language.* Unabridged ed. New York: Random House.

Stern, Stephen. 1977. "Ethnic Folklore and the Folklore of Ethnicity." *Western Folklore*, 36(January):7-32.

Sumner, William Graham. 1906. *Folkways: A Study of the Sociological Importance of Usages, Manners, Customs, Mores, and Morals.* [Rpt. 1960, New York: Mentor/New American Library].

Tamony, Peter. 1965. "Chinaman's Chance." *Western Folklore*, 24(July): 202-5.

—— 1977. "Keeks, Kikes, Kooks and Courrèges." *Maledicta*, 1(Winter): 269-82.

Tarpley, Fred. 1970. *From Blinky to Blue-John: A Word Atlas of Northeast Texas.* Wolfe City, Texas: University Press.

Taylor, Ronald L. 1979. "Black Ethnicity and the Persistence of Ethnogenesis." *American Journal of Sociology*, 84(May):1401-23.

Taylor, Sharon Henderson. 1974. "Terms for Low Intelligence." *American Speech*, 49(Fall-Winter):197-207.

Thernstrom, Stephan, Ann Orlov, and Oscar Handlin, eds. 1980. *Harvard Encyclopedia of American Ethnic Groups.* Cambridge: Belknap Press of Harvard University Press.

Thorne, Barrie and Nancy Henley. 1975. "Difference and Dominance: An Overview of Language, Gender, and Society." In B. Thorne and N. Henley, eds., *Language and Sex*, pp. 5-42. Rowley, Mass.: Newbury House.

Thornton, Richard H. 1912. *An American Glossary: Being an Attempt to Illustrate Certain Americanisms Upon Historical Principles.* 3 vols. Vols. 1 and 2, Philadelphia: J.P. Lippincott. Vol. 3 published in *Dialect Notes*, vol. 6 (1931-1939), Madison: American Dialect Society [rpt., n.d., University of Alabama Press].

Tindall, George Brown. 1976. *The Ethnic Southerners.* Baton Rouge: Louisiana State University Press.

Toll, Robert C. 1974. *Blacking Up: The Minstrel Show in Nineteenth-Century America.* New York: Oxford University Press.

Trudeau, Pierre Elliott. 1977. A solicited letter to the editor under the heading, "Mr. Trudeau, What's a 'Canuck'?" *New York Times*, February 25, p. 23.

Trudgill, Peter. 1972. "Sex, Covert Prestige, and Linguistic Change in the Urban British English of Norwich." *Language in Society*, 1(October):179-95.

U.S. Bureau of the Census. 1913. *Thirteenth Census of the United States: 1910. Vol. 1. Population. General Report and Analysis.* Washington, D.C.: U.S. Government Printing Office.

—— 1933. *Fifteenth Census of the United States: 1930. Population, vol. 2, General Report. Statistics by Subjects.* Washington, D.C.: U.S. Government Printing Office.

—— 1973. *Census of the Population: 1970. Subject Reports. Final Report PC(2)-1A. National Origin and Language.* Washington, D.C.: U.S. Government Printing Office.

—— 1975. *Historical Statistics of the United States, Colonial Times to 1970.* Bicentennial ed. Washington, D.C.: U.S. Government Printing Office.

Van Patten, Nathan. 1931. "The Vocabulary of the American Negro as Set Forth in Contemporary Literature." *American Speech*, 7(October):24-31.

Vizetelly, Frank H. 1929. "The Origin of 'Gringo' " (a letter to the editor). *New York Times*, September 29, p. E-5.

Wall, C. Edward and Edward Przebienda. 1969. *Words and Phrases Index.* 3 vols. Ann Arbor: Pierian.

Wax, Murray L. 1971. *Indian Americans: Unity and Diversity.* Englewood Cliffs, N.J.: Prentice-Hall.

Weekley, Ernest. 1932. *Words and Names.* London: John Murray.

Weingarten, Joseph A. 1954. *An American Dictionary of Slang and Colloquial Speech.* New York: published by the author.

Welsch, Roger L. 1967. "American Numbskull Tales: The Polack Joke." *Western Folklore*, 26(July):183-86.

Wentworth, Harold and Stuart Berg Flexner. 1975. *Dictionary of American Slang.* 2d supplemented ed. New York: Thomas Y. Crowell.

Wescott, Roger W. 1971. "Labio-Velarity and Derogation in English: A Study in Phonosemic Correlation." *American Speech*, 46(Spring-Summer):123-37.

Weseen, Maurice H. 1934. *A Dictionary of American Slang.* New York: Thomas Y. Crowell.

Wirth, Louis. 1928. *The Ghetto.* Chicago: University of Chicago Press.

—— 1938. "Urbanism as a Way of Life." *American Journal of Sociology*, 44(July):3-24.

Wolfe, Tom. 1968. "You and Your Big Mouth: How the Honks and Wonks Reveal the Phonetic Truth about Status." *New York*, April 8, pp. 59-61.

Yancey, William L., Eugene P. Ericksen and Richard N. Juliani. 1976. "Emergent Ethnicity: A Review and Reformulation." *American Sociological Review*, 41(June):391-403.

INDEX